Massachusetts State Police Salisbury Beach

1935 Salisbury Beach – A. McCabe, Charles Furze, A. Chaisson, J. Blake – W. Killen Cook Albie

Salisbury Beach Detail
Sub-Station A-5
1933 to 1995

Ronald J. Guilmette

P.O. Box 238
Morley, MO 63767
(573) 472-9800
www.acclaimpress.com

Book & Cover Design: Rodney Atchley

ISBN: 978-1-956027-42-6 / 1-956027-42-4

First Printing: 2024
Printed in the United States of America
10 9 8 7 6 5 4 3 2 1

This publication was produced using available information.
The publisher regrets it cannot assume responsibility for errors or omissions.

CONTENTS

Acknowledgments 4

Introduction - Salisbury Beach State Reservation 5

The Thirties 7

The Forties 13

The Fifties 18

The Sixties 26

The Seventies 33

The Eighties 37

The Nineties 41

Epilogue 43

Camaraderie 45

Index 47

American flag, Marine Corps flag, and the Irish flag flown daily over Salisbury Beach, by Lieutenant Richard J. "Red" McDonald, MSP Retired ... RIP my friend.

ACKNOWLEDGMENTS

This book was prepared for the Massachusetts Department of State Police and the Massachusetts State Police Museum and Learning Center to memorialize more than 220 Troopers who served at the Salisbury Beach Barracks from 1933 to 1995.

The research and writing was completed by museum researcher and author Ronald J. Guilmette, Lt. Colonel Massachusetts State Police, retired.

Assistance was provided by the following public institutions and individuals who are acknowledged here: Joe's Playland Salisbury Beach, Salisbury Public Library, Newburyport Public Library, the Massachusetts State Police Museum and Learning Center, Massachusetts State Library State House Boston, Town of Salisbury Assessors Office, Massachusetts State Police Public Affairs Office, and Haverhill Public Library.

A special thank you to the following individuals for providing photos and/or information for this book: Steve Gravelle, Richard Connelly, Hervey Cote, Arthur Ober, Dennis Bertulli, Steve Alvino, Eddie Amodeo, Don Kennefick, Bob Krom, Ed Johnson III, Ed Horton, Dave Procopio, Jim Crump, Peter Mazeikus, Gail McVeigh, Patrick Silva, Robert T. Jackson, Tom McNulty, Kristen Ryan, Bob McKeon, Dick & Sue Belanger, Beverly Donahue Barnard, Dianne Masiello, Brian Eng, and Henry E. Sullivan.

Colonel John E. Mawn
Appointed February 17, 2023

Captain/Executive Officer Charles T. Beaupre implemented the French & Electric Blue uniforms in 1933.

Introduction

On June 10, 1931, The Massachusetts State Legislature passed Chapter 0442 authorizing the Commissioner of Conservation to take by eminent domain certain parcels of land at Salisbury Beach and establish a state reservation trust fund, and appropriated $50,000 to be assessed to the cities and towns of the commonwealth.

I. A parcel of land bordering upon the Atlantic ocean, and extending from the Merrimack River on the south to the Massachusetts–New Hampshire boundary on the north, and between the line of mean low water of said ocean on the east and the easterly established boundary lines of the lots abutting said parcel of land on the west.

In 1933, the Massachusetts State Police established a substation at Salisbury Beach, designated as A-5 and later changed to A-6. The state police rented a cottage to billet the officers at 308 North End Boulevard for $400 for the remainder of the summer. The cottage was known as the Hall cottage, owned by Gertrude and George Hall. The barracks was assigned one cruiser and motorcycles and a teletype was installed. According to the July 15, 1933 edition of the Newburyport Herald, "The new barracks will have the whole-hearted support of the Salisbury townspeople, who have often in the past petitioned the State House for state police protection during the summer months when it is not unusual for crowds of 40,000 to flock there on weekends. Of late years, it has been suspected that gangsters and petty criminal were nesting in Salisbury

The Hall Cottage, now # 298 North End Boulevard, is in the photo on the right. (2024 photo)

and one of the first tasks of the troops will be to clean out any "public enemies" who have established hideaways at the beach." Additionally, to add to the on-going crime problems, in 1927 the Salisbury Police Chief, Harold Congdon, two selectmen and two police officers were arrested and jailed for Rum Running.

In 1935, the troopers moved to a new location at 166 North End Boulevard across the street from the Star of the Sea Catholic Church. The property was owned by the James P. Smith family, and one of the daughters, Elizabeth Coulson

The Smith home is the large house behind the garage, and the small house to the right was rented to the state police for a summer barracks, Memorial Day to Labor Day from 1935 until 1945. (Photo taken in 2021)

Smith, would later marry one of the Troopers stationed at the beach, Eugene L. Murphy, who later served as the Salisbury Police Chief.

The state police would occupy two more locations during its sixty-plus year presence at Salisbury Beach: the Central Avenue Military Fire Control Tower from 1946 to 1950 and 451 North End Boulevard from 1951 to 1971.

The year 1933 was also a historic year for the State Police because it signified the first change in uniforms from the original 1921 forest green surplus military uniforms to the legendary French and Electric Blue. Troopers wore the heavy wool uniforms and high boots year round until a comfortable summer uniform was adopted in 1967, and they began wearing the campaign cover in 1964.

BEACH QUARTERS ARE RENTED FOR STATE POLICE

(Copeland News Service)

State House, Boston, July 13.— State police will patrol the new State Reservation at Salisbury Beach.

Samuel York, state commissioner of conservation, requested Daniel Needham, state commissioner of public safety, for the troopers.

Six men will be assigned, it is understood, and this afternoon the executive council approved a contract for quarters for these men, a cottage located at 308 North End Boulevard. The cottage will be rented for the remainder of the 1933 season, with the state police "tenants at will." The rental for that period being $400.

14-MILE CHASE ENDS AS PURSUED CRASHES

Special Dispatch to the Globe

SALISBURY BEACH, Aug 6—Chased 14 miles by the State Police and fired at twice, John Kelley, 24, of East High st, Newbury, was arrested this morning on three charges after the automobile in which he fled had struck a stonewall.

Kelley passed through Salisbury sq shortly before noon. State officers Rich and Ford ordered him to stop, instead he stepped on the gas and the chase began. One of the shots pierced his windshield.

When taken into custody he was given medical treatment. He is charged with driving under the influence, operating a vehicle so as to endanger, and refusing to stop when signaled by a police officer.

JAIL SENTENCES FOR SALISBURY RUM RING MEN

SALEM, Dec. 1, 1927—(AP)—Prison sentences ranging from two to two and one-half years and fines of $1000 were imposed by Judge Joseph F. Quinn today upon Harold F. Congdon, former Salisbury Beach chief of police, and four others convicted of charges in connection with the so-called Salisbury Beach liquor conspiracy case.

Congdon, convicted on two charges, received the heaviest sentence. He was given two and one-half years in the house of correction, and fined $1000 on each charge, that of conspiracy to violate the liquor law and conspiracy to bribe, but the prison sentences were fixed to run concurrently so that his actual term will amount only to two and one-half years with fines totaling $2000.

Each of the others, Ruell S. Getchell and Everett R. George, former Salisbury selectmen, and Warren S. Frothingham and Howard F. George, former police officers, were sentenced to two years in the house of correction and to pay fines of $1000.

The court granted a stay of execution pending the filing of exceptions.

BEACH SUB-STATION OF STATE POLICE WILL BE OPENED MONDAY

Trooper Arthur V. Ford Will Be Acting Corporal—Five Others Assigned For Duty at Salisbury

Salisbury Beach Reservation

The establishment of a State reservation at Salisbury Beach at an expense of $50,000 is proposed in a bill filed by Representatives Thomas J. Lane of Lawrence and Carl A. Woekel of Methuen.

THE THIRTIES

1933 — The first officers assigned to the detail in July of 1933 were: Arthur V. Ford, Acting Corporal; Patrick T. Ridge, Senior Trooper; William B. Killen, Donat LaCasse, Walter P. Burke, and Francis C. Hannigan. On July 15, 1933, a teletype machine was installed at the new station at Salisbury Beach with a direct connection to the State Police switchboard at Framingham. The Troopers were billeted at a summer cottage at 308 North End Boulevard. Arthur Ford and Walter Burke retired as Corporals, Patrick Ridge and Francis Hanigan retired as Troopers, Donat LaCasse retired as a Sergeant and William Killen retired as a Lieutenant.

1934 — Assigned for the Summer of 1934 were: John J. Powers (OIC), Thomas J. Qualters, George F. Fielding, Arthur F. Chasson, and Robert B. Smith. The Troopers were again billeted at 308 North End Boulevard. Thomas Qualters had a letter of recommendation in his file from Knute Rockne, the famous Notre Dame football coach. Qualters left the state police in 1935 to become the personal bodyguard for President Franklin D. Roosevelt. Powers, Smith and Fielding all retired as Troopers.

Arthur Ford,
17th RTT, 1927.

Patrick Ridge,
18th RTT, 1927.

William B. Killen,
23rd RTT, 1927.

Walter Burke,
20th RTT, 1928.

Francis O. Hanigan,
24th RTT, 1931.

Donat A. LaCasse,
24th RTT, 1931.

Early 1930 Cruiser & Indian Motorcycle

John J. Powers,
10th RTT, 1924.

Robert B. Smith,
24th RTT, 1931.

George F. Fielding,
22nd RTT, 1930.

Thomas J. Qualters,
25th RTT, 1933.

Arthur Chaisson,
22nd RTT, 1930.

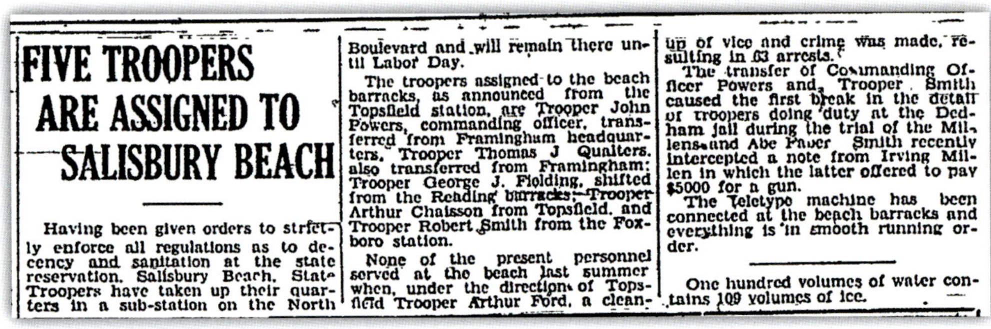

FIVE TROOPERS ARE ASSIGNED TO SALISBURY BEACH

Having been given orders to strictly enforce all regulations as to decency and sanitation at the state reservation, Salisbury Beach, State Troopers have taken up their quarters in a sub-station on the North Boulevard and will remain there until Labor Day.

The troopers assigned to the beach barracks, as announced from the Topsfield station, are Trooper John Powers, commanding officer, transferred from Framingham headquarters, Trooper Thomas J. Qualters, also transferred from Framingham; Trooper George J. Fielding, shifted from the Reading barracks; Trooper Arthur Chaisson from Topsfield, and Trooper Robert Smith from the Foxboro station.

None of the present personnel served at the beach last summer when, under the direction of Topsfield Trooper Arthur Ford, a clean-up of vice and crime was made, resulting in 63 arrests.

The transfer of Commanding Officer Powers and Trooper Smith caused the first break in the detail of troopers doing duty at the Dedham jail during the trial of the Millens and Abe Faber. Smith recently intercepted a note from Irving Millen in which the latter offered to pay $5000 for a gun.

The Teletype machine has been connected at the beach barracks and everything is in smooth running order.

One hundred volumes of water contains 109 volumes of ice.

Eleanor and President Franklin D. Roosevelt with former Trooper Thomas J. Qualters, 1936.

Arthur F. Chaisson, 22nd RTT, 1930 on an Indian motorcycle.

SIX MEN IN STOLEN AUTO ARE CAUGHT BY TROOPER AFTER CHASE

Three of Group Also Wanted by the State Police for Series of Breaks in Wilmington

State Trooper Arthur F. Chaisson of the Salisbury Beach barracks decided that six young men who went past him in an automobile on the Lafayette highway in Salisbury yesterday morning at 1.30 o'clock, looked suspicious, so he pursued and overtook them, to find out that they had stolen a car and that three of the group were wanted by the state police of the Reading station.

He arrested the group for using an automobile without authority. They are Albert DeVito, 23 Emerson street, Wakefield; Joseph Keough, Shawsheen avenue, Wilmington; his brother, Edward Keough, alias Edward De-Cota, same address; Henry Champa, 3 Lamolie street, North Woburn, Harold Prosper, 39 Charles street, Wakefield, and Charles Beighley, 69 Albion street, Wakefield.

DeVito and the Keough brothers are wanted by the state police in connection with a series of breaks at Silver Lake in Wilmington. They were turned over to the Wakefield police for prosecution, after which the local police will enter the case. Sergeant John J Cote and four Wakefield officers returned them to that town yesterday.

The automobile was the property of William C. Vest, 19 Byron street, Wakefield.

Some of the young men are said to be members of the Charlestown loop gang, who drive at reckless speed in stolen cars and defy the police

---

Charged with assault on State trooper Thomas J. Qualters of the Salisbury Beach barracks, Lawrence P. Eaton, Seabrook, N H, was given a 60-day suspended jail term. On a drunkenness count he paid a $15 fine. He was arrested Sunday evening, following a disturbance at Salisbury Beach.

Two Men Fined on Charges of Assaulting Each Other

Amesbury, June 25—Harry A Mencis, 38. of 87 Arlington street, Haverhill, and Nils L. Olson, 31 of 8 Henry street, this town, were each found guilty of charges of assault and battery when arraigned before Judge Charles I Pettingell in Saturday's session of the second district court Mencis was fined $25 while Olson's assessment was $5. The Haverhill defendant appealed and was ordered to post bonds of $200.

The complaints were brought as the result of an alleged fracas at Salisbury Beach Friday evening. State Trooper George Fielding of the Salisbury Beach barracks prosecuted.

Olson testified that he was at Salisbury Beach with his sister, Mrs. Florence A. Mencis and her 9-year-old daughter Olson told the court that the little girl argued as to the control of Mencis argued as to the control, with the Haverhill man striking the first blow, according to the local man's story

It was revealed during the court trial that Mrs. Mencis had been awarded the custody of the child by order of the Lawrence probate court.

Other witnesses for Olson included Mrs. Mencis and Andrew J Pendergast 30 of 28 Winter street, this town. The latter testified that he did not see the fight, but came along shortly afterward Mencis cross-examined each witness and had to be warned several times by the court as to the method of questioning

The Haverhill man took the stand and declared that Olson was responsible for the fight His testimony was corroborated by Raymond W O'Shea, also of Haverhill, who was Mencis' companion

In passing sentence the court declared that inasmuch as Mrs. Mencis has been awarded custody of the little girl she had full control over the child.

St. Jean Society Attends Mass

Amesbury, June 25.—Members of the St Jean de Baptiste society of the Sacred Heart parish observed an annual custom in attending mass in a body at 10.30 yesterday morning The

---

Court Unusually Busy This Month

Amesbury, Sept 24.—Nearly 200 cases will have been tried in the second district court here in September one of the busiest months in the court's history. according to Clerk Earl M Nelson.

Many traffic violations are scheduled for trial Monday, Tuesday, and Thursday of this week, with a total of 70 to be heard between now and the first of the month.

Activities of the state police of the Salisbury Beach barracks have been an important factor in increasing the court dockets Left-of-day violations are the cause of the largest percentage of complaints

---

STATE TROOPER IS INJURED IN CRASH WITH HUGE TRUCK

John C. Blake, Jr., Taken to Hospital for Treatment of Injuries Received Here This Morning

Hospital treatment was required for State Trooper John C. Blake, Jr., 23, of the Topsfield barracks, who was injured this forenoon when his motorcycle crashed against the side of a big truck that made an unexpected right turn into the driveway of the Towle Manufacturing Company, 266 Merrimac street.

Trooper Blake was riding along Merrimac street on his way to the Amesbury district court and was following the truck, which was operated by Robert J. Lynch, 23, 103 Sheridan street, Chicopee Falls. As the truck neared the driveway, which is opposite Broad street, Lynch pulled toward the left and the policeman assumed he intended to turn the truck into Broad street.

Instead, the truckman turned the truck toward the Towle driveway and Trooper Blake, who was still in his right lane, was unable to stop his motorcycle before it struck against the side of the van. He was knocked to the ground and suffered many bruises and his uniform was cut at the knees. His motorcycle also was damaged.

Henry O. Chase, 28 Woodland street, who was driving past and witnessed the accident, took Trooper Blake to the Anna Jaques hospital, where his injuries were treated, but he was not required to remain.

A few months ago Trooper Blake was in a more serious accident. He had halted a driver at night because the man seemed suspicious, and while he was standing outside the car—the motorist slammed a door shut, imprisoning Blake's hands. The officer was dragged nearly a quarter of a mile before the driver opened the door without slackening speed and let him fall to the roadside. Later the man's identity was established and he was sentenced in court.

ALLEGED AUTO THIEF TAKEN AFTER CHASE

Two Troopers, One Off Duty, Nab Rockport Man in Sunday Night Crowd at Salisbury

Two state troopers, one of whom was off duty and in plain clothes at the time, chased two alleged automobile thieves through a crowd at Salisbury Beach last night and caught one of them. A search is being made for the other and it is expected he will be taken into custody soon.

SALISBURY PATROL STARTS TOMORROW

Barracks of State Police Opening Earlier

TOPSFIELD, May 29—The State patrol barracks at Salisbury Beach will open there tomorrow opposite the Star of the Sea Chapel, for the Summer season. The barracks are opening this year about a month earlier than usual due to the heavy traffic. The barracks will be equipped with teletype printer, cruising cars and other up-to-date police apparatus, and the barracks will continue to function through Labor Day.

At Topsfield today the State announced the following personnel for the Salisbury barracks: commanding officer Charles F. Furze, senior man, who is transferred from the Concord barracks; patrolman Arthur E. McCabe, also from Concord; troopers Arthur F. Chaisson and John C. Blake from Topsfield and William B. Killen from the Foxboro barracks.

Arthur McCabe, 24th RTT, 1931.

The 1935 beach detail, seated L to R: Arthur E. McCabe, Charles F. Furze, Arthur F. Chaisson. Standing: John C. Blake, Mess Boy/Cook Albie Woick, and William B. Killen. For the summer of 1935 the state rented a different barracks located at 166 North End Boulevard, Route 1A, across from the Star of the Sea Church. "Mess Boy/Cook" Alexander "Albie" Woick would later be among the first to receive the agency's highest civilian award in 1971, the Massachusetts State Police Medal for Meritorious Service. Furze would rise to the rank of Captain and Blake would become the first ever to hold the rank of Lt. Colonel in 1958. Chaisson would retire as a sergeant after twenty years of service in 1950, and William Killen retired as a Lieutenant in 1950.

ANDOVER MOTORIST FINED, DRIVING UNDER INFLUENCE

AMESBURY, Aug 14—Fred Brewer of Andover was fined $50 when found guilty of driving while under the influence of liquor by Judge Charles I. Pettingell in 2d District Court yesterday.

He was arrested in Salisbury Saturday by Corp Charles F. Furze of the State Police and Arthur E. McCabe, State trooper, attached to the Salisbury Beach barracks.

The 1936 beach detail consisted of the following officers: Charles F. Furze (Acting Corporal), Arthur F. Chaisson, John C. Blake, Roland Savage, Herbert S. Berglund, and John W. Collins. Roland Savage retired as a Trooper in 1941, John Collins as a Captain in 1953, and Herbert Berglund left to become the Chief of Police in Easton, Massachusetts and served there until 1958.

Herbert S. Berglund, 20th RTT, 1928.

Roland W. Savage, 25th RTT, 1933.

John W. Collins, 20th RTT, 1928.

Berglund on Indian motorcycle

TROOPER'S KNOWLEDGE OF FIRST AID SAVES GUARDSMAN'S LIFE

John C. Blake of State Police Renders Valuable Aid to Vernon Smith, Badly Cut in Auto Crash

STATE TROOPER IS "ARRESTED" BY MAN HE SOUGHT TO TAKE

Law Student Must Explain Conduct to Court, Which He Must Face on Two Charges

State Trooper Roland W. Savage of the Salisbury Beach barracks, had the unique experience of being "arrested" by a prisoner Saturday afternoon. Full details of the odd affair are to be aired Wednesday in the Amesbury district court. The man who "arrested" Savage is Elston Eaton, 25, 34 Main street, Belfast Maine, a Columbia University law student.

Trooper Savage was on duty on the Lafayette road near Brown's park when he halted Eaton for speeding and placed him under arrest because the violation was allegedly a flagrant one. The officer told the Maine man to precede him to the station, but Eaton is alleged to have grabbed him by the shoulder and said to Savage.

"I place you under arrest. I know my law."

The officer told him not to argue there, but to proceed to the lockup. Eaton allegedly told him "No, you precede me because you are my prisoner."

Trooper Savage then went to enter the automobile to drive it to the Salisbury station, but was not allowed to do so by Eaton. The next thing that occurred was a wrestling match.

The two rolled all over the highway and traffic was stopped, a crowd gathered to watch the pair apply various holds, and one of the spectators informed the barracks. Before the arrival of Troopers John Collins and Herbert Berglund, the wrestling match was over and Eaton had a second charge against him, that of assault on an officer.

The man said he was enroute to Boston to see a brother, who was about to be graduated from the Harvard Law School.

STATE POLICE TO PATROL ROADS TO N. H. LINE

The state police are installed in their summer barracks at Salisbury Beach and today commenced their duties of patrolling the roads from Newburyport to the New Hampshire line. They will also cover the roads leading to Amesbury and will do police work along the beach.

Acting Corporal Charles F. Furze said he and his officers would co-operate with the Salisbury police. The Salisbury station is to be used to hold prisoners.

Trooper John Collins will be senior officer under Acting Corporal Furze.

STATE POLICE REOPEN SUBSTATION AT BEACH

SALISBURY BEACH, May 27—The state police substation here was opened today and troopers began patrolling the highways from Newburyport to the New Hampshire line.

Arrests made by the troopers this year will be prosecuted in the Amesbury Court.

Trooper Charles F. Furze, who was in charge of the Summer station last year, has been named acting corporal again.

Other troopers sent here were: Arthur F. Chaisson and John C. Blake of the Topsfield barracks; Roland Savage of the Andover barracks; Herbert S. Berglund, Foxboro, and John Collins, Concord.

The 1937 Salisbury Beach detail, front steps: Mess Boy/Cook Albie Woick. Officers seated L to R: Leward L. "Joe" Bean, Charles F. Furze (OIC), and Daniel L. Jacobs. Standing: John C. Blake, Charles J. Collins, Robert F. Bourbeau. Charles Collins was shot and killed in the line of duty at Byfield, Massachusetts on May 19, 1942. His assailant was shot and killed at the scene by Trooper George C. Edwards. Bourbeau and Furze would both rise to the rank of Captain, and Blake would become the first ever to hold the rank of Lt. Colonel in 1958. Joe Bean left the state police in 1937 and went to work for GE in New York, and Jacobs left the state police in 1939 to start his own lobster and crab business in Gloucester.

STATE TROOPER BEAN SOON TO LEAVE FORCE

State Trooper Leward Bean of the Salisbury Beach barracks, was born in Nashua, N. H., on November 10, 1907. In 1911, when four years old, he moved to Haverhill where he received his early education. While attending Haverhill High school, he was prominent in athletics, playing tackle for three years in football, and being an outfield star in baseball. During his last year of football he was captain of the Brown and Gold eleven.

Upon graduation, Trooper Bean entered the General Electric Engineering school where he studied to be a sales engineer. Next Friday he will leave the state police force to go to the General Electric company in Schenectady, N. Y., where he will be employed as sales engineer in the local office.

After graduating from the engineering school, Trooper Bean took the examination for the state police and finished well up among the applicants, and was assigned to the state police recruit school in Bridgewater, where he was graduated with honors. His first assignment after graduation was to Troop A in Foxboro, then to Andover and Topsfield. This is his first year at the beach.

Trooper Bean, aside from being well-known at the Beach has served on many important details, among them being the famous Millen-Faber case at the Dedham jail.

MALDEN BOY ARRESTED IN CHASE AT SALISBURY

NEWBURYPORT, July 15—After a chase of over a mile along the Salisbury Beach boulevard last night, a 15-year-old Malden boy was arrested by state trooper Charles J. Collins, charged with stealing an automobile, the property of Henry J. Keefe, superintendent of highways. It was stolen from his garage, State st.

Trooper Collins sighted the stolen car in Salisbury sq and chased it to the north end of the beach, where he placed the youth under arrest.

STATE TROOPER TO WED NEW YORK ENTERTAINER

NEWBURYPORT, June 29—The engagement of State Trooper John C. Blake Jr of the Salisbury Beach

MISS SHIRLEY BOSTON

barracks and Miss Shirley Boston, New York night club entertainer, formerly of Haverhill, was announced today. They will be married in the Autumn.

Miss Boston is a daughter of Mrs Elizabeth Boston of 300 West 49th st, New York. Blake, who has been in the State Police service three years, is a son of Mr and Mrs John C. Blake of Roslindale. His father is a lieutenant in the Boston Police Department.

The 1938 Salisbury Beach detail consisted of the following personnel: Charles F. Furze (OIC), Troopers John C. Blake, Robert Bourbeau, Frank Geist, and John H. Fallon. John Fallon retired as a Trooper in 1942 and Frank Geist as a Lieutenant in 1955.

John Fallon,
27th RTT, 1936.

Frank Geist,
20th RTT, 1938.

Robert Bourbeau,
26th RTT, 1934.

Assign Corporal Furze To Shelburne Falls

BOSTON — Charles F. Furze of Fall River has been promoted to the rank of corporal in the state police by Public Safety Commissioner Eugene M. McSweeney and sent to the Shelburne Falls barracks to be in command. For the past four years, as senior private, he has been commanding officer at the Salisbury Beach station of the division during the summer season. Since that station closed this year, he has been stationed at Wrentham.

Charles F. Furze,
20th RTT, 1928.

Trooper John C. Blake leaning over the handlebars, and Charles Furze behind the motorcycle at summer station, Salisbury, ca. 1938.

The 1939 Salisbury Beach detail consisted of the following personnel: Michael Shea (OIC), Edward J. Sullivan, Frank Geist, Donat Lacasse, Robert Bourbeau, and George C. Edwards. Edward Sullivan and George C. Edwards retired as Sergeants and Michael Shea as a Trooper in 1950.

Edward J. Sullivan, 27th RTT, 1936.

Michael J. Shea, 17th RTT, 1927.

Robert Bourbeau, 26th RTT, 1934.

FIVE TROOPERS FOR SALISBURY

Makeup of the detail that will serve at the Salisbury Beach summer barracks. which opens tomorrow. was disclosed today by state police headquarters Trooper Michael Shea now of the Concord barracks. will be in charge Given transfers to Salisbury Beach with him were Patrolmen George Clinton Edwards of Topsfield barracks. Donat Lacasse of Concord barracks Edward Sullivan of Framingham barracks and Robert F Bourbeau of Wrentham barracks

Troopers Edwards and Bourbeau have served at the Beach before. Lacasse was at Topsfield a few years ago

THE PROMOTION OF Charles F Furze from patrolman to corporal in the state police was pleasing to many people in this section because the burly officer has made a lot of friends in his service as officer in charge of the Salisbury Beach summer barracks They would like to see him in charge at the beach next year. too.

"Trunks Only" Barred at Salisbury Beach

SALISBURY BEACH, July 10— For the first time the Town Fathers are campaigning against partial nudity of bathers who walk through the crowded streets. "Any man seen walking on Broadway or elsewhere wearing nothing but trunks is going to be arrested," declared Harold F. Congdon, chief of police and chairman of the Selectmen, today.

"Furthermore, no man or woman is going to be allowed to parade around in a bathing suit. In these cases we will give a first warning, but parading in trunks only is forbidden and there will be no warning given," said Chief Congdon.

Suspended Sentence for C. C. C. Trio

AMESBURY, June 9 — Three Greater Boston youths, attached to the Salisbury Beach C. C. C. camp, today were found guilty, following a hearing before Judge Charles I. Pettingill in the Second District Court here, on charges of breaking and entering and larceny in the night time.

They were Daniel J. Hunt, 18, of Meridian st., East Boston; Daniel A. Roche, 17, of Cherry st., West Newton, and James J. Costa, 18, of 4th st., East Cambridge.

They were arrested by State Troopers Michael Shea and Donat A. Lacasse of the Salisbury Beach barracks in connection with a break May 3 at a sea grill on Beach road, Salisbury, operated by Chester Cole. Cigars and cigarettes were taken in the break.

The youths pleaded not guilty, were found guilty and each was given a six months' suspended sentence. Each was placed on probation for two years.

FORMER SALISBURY OFFICIALS SERVED 21 MONTHS OF JAIL TERM

Former Selectmen Ruell S. Getchell and Everett R. George and former Patrolmen Warren S. Frothingham and Howard F George, all of Salisbury have been released from the Essex county jail after serving 21 months of 27 months' sences. There were released by the county commissioners, who had studied the case with Probation Officer Charles Salisbury of Andover All had been imprisoned on liquor charges in the famous Salisbury Beach liquor conspiracy case. All four, were sentenced to two

years' imprisonment in the house of correction and were fined $1000 each on Dec. 1, 1927. They were unable to pay and took the poor debtor's oath and were given an additional three months to serve

At the time of their release the four men had been eligible for parole for several months.

Harold S. Congdon, former police chief of Salisbury. who was fined $2000 and received a sentence of two and a half years on a charge of conspiracy to violate the liquor law. is still serving his sentence in Lawrence jail.

Salisbury officials complete jail sentence, 1930.

THE FORTIES

The 1940 Salisbury Beach detail consisted of the following personnel: Michael Shea (OIC), George Edwards, Robert Bourbeau, Frank Geist, Edward Sullivan, and Albie Woick (Cook).

The 1941 Salisbury Beach detail consisted of the following personnel: Michael Shea (OIC), George Edwards, John C. Blake, Julian Zuk, Gustave R. Swanson, and Albie Woick

(Cook). Gus Swanson retired as a Captain and Julian Zuk as a Lt. Colonel.

Because of World War II manpower shortage on the state police, there was no Salisbury Beach Detail from the summer of 1942 until it was started up again in 1946. Patrols, when available, were sent from the Topsfield Barracks, but the loss of the assigned detail was sorely missed by the townspeople.

AVIATOR WHO SCARED BEACH CROWD FINED $25

An aviator who flew an estimated 30 to 40 feet above the shoreline at Salisbury Beach on the afternoon of June 29 and frightened many persons was fined $25 in the Amesbury district court today by Judge Charles I Pettingell He was charged with a violation of the laws dealing with vehicles propelled by motors. The defendant was Paul F Fryer, 25, of Orchard street, Dedham

The number of the airplane was taken by State Trooper George C Edwards of the Salisbury Beach barracks at the time of the offence When the operator's identity had been established, Trooper Michael Shea, in charge of the beach barracks, went to Canton airport and placed Fryer under arrest Superintendent J Andrew Walsh, in charge of the state reservation at the beach was associated with the state police in the investigation.

Gustave Swanson, 28th RTT, 1938.

Julian Zuk (28th RTT, 1938) with Governor Bradford

Bragging Results in Fine For Assault

Amesbury, June 26—Ralph Blaisdell, 18, of 6 Ocean street, Newburyport, bragged his way into a $10 fine for assault and battery, imposed by Judge Charles I Pettingell in the second district court here today

Blaisdell the story goes was with a group of other youths who were involved in trouble at a Salisbury Beach amusement place about two weeks ago One of the youths got away

Yesterday Blaisdell was in a lunch-cart at the beach telling about how he got away State police in quick time had a warrant for his arrest by Troopers Frank W Geist and George Clinton Edwards.

NEWBURYPORT DAILY NEWS
AND NEWBURYPORT HERALD

VOL. 65, NO. 117   NEWBURYPORT, MASS. WEDNESDAY, MAY 20, 1942   6 PAGES   THREE CENTS

DRINK-CRAZED BYFIELD MAN KILLS TROOPER AND IS SLAIN

R.A.F. in Fierce Raid on Mannheim   State Officer Charles J. Collins Is Victim of Bullets Fired By Edward L. Rogers

Great German Industrial City | LOCAL GIRL TO RECEIVE DEGREE | F. D. R. HONORS HERO WHO LED RAID ON TOKIO

Charles Collins
EOW, May 20, 1942

★ ★ ★
TRIBUTE TO TROOPERS—Sympathy to his widow and admiration for the bravery of State Trooper Charles J. Collins of Beverly were expressed in a resolution adopted by the Governor's Council. The officer was fatally wounded in a gun duel with a Byfield man Wednesday morning. In another resolution Trooper George C. Edwards of Haverhill was commended for risking his life in slaying the gunman.
★ ★ ★

George C. Edwards

In 1943, in the midst of World War II, the U.S. Government built fourteen concrete observation towers along the Maine, New Hampshire and Massachusetts seacoast to defend the Portsmouth Harbor and the busy military industry facility at the Portsmouth Naval Shipyard. Each tower had direct telephone contact with the gun batteries at Fort Dearborn (now Odiorne State Park) to report any sightings of enemy ships or aircraft. The New Hampshire and Massachusetts Towers were: Pulpit Rock Tower, which is still standing in Rye Beach, New Hampshire; Rye Ledge Tower at Rye Beach, NH, which is no longer standing; Boars Head Tower on Boars Head at Hampton Beach, NH, which is still standing; Salisbury Beach Tower at Salisbury Beach, MA, which is no longer standing; and The Plum Island station located on Plum Island, Newbury, MA, no longer standing.

The Salisbury Tower was a two and one-half story wooden cottage with a three-story concrete tower that was completed in October 1943 on a leased 0.65-acre site (Site 1A) as a Base-End Station for Fort Dearborn. It was located approximately 200 yards North of the present-day Salisbury Beach Amusement Center in front of the line of cottages located in front of 60 Central Avenue. After the war, the federal government

TROOPER EDWARDS JOINS THE NAVY

The undermanned Topsfield barracks has lost another man with the decision of State Trooper George C Edwards to enter the navy Edwards, a Haverhill man with more than a dozen years' experience in the state force, was granted a leave of absence yesterday and enlisted in the naval reserve, having made application some time ago. He went to Boston yesterday to be sworn in as a chief boatswain. Edwards, 36, has been second in command at Topsfield for several years and is a former assistant coach of football at Newburyport High school.

FACT THAT THE state police barracks at Salisbury Beach was not open this summer undoubtedly is a matter to be regretted, but it was the result of wartime conditions The state police force has been considerably depleted, as many members have gone into the armed services, others into federal law enforcement agencies and some into private employment The nearest permanent barracks to Salisbury Beach, the one at Topsfield, has been undermanned for some time because of the wartime conditions, and other stations have felt the lack of men. Possibly next season the state force may be built up to sufficient size to allow the re-opening of the Salisbury Beach sub-station

---

CLOSING OF STATE BARRACKS IS DEPLORED

(Continued from Page One)

Salisbury Those who live here are orderly, and law-abiding Most of the transients are decent, good people But we have had too much hoodlumism, too much laxity, and too many questionable characters at large here this year to make us feel that the absence of the barracks was not a factor to be deeply regretted I won't go into details, for I know you understand what I mean Most of the objectionable features would not have occurred if the state police were established here in residence, as they were for the past 10 years

"Thirdly, Father Lee and I were never given an opportunity to voice our opinion about the need of a state police barracks here prior to the closing of them Where grave moral issues are at stake, it would seem that the clergy should have been consulted The first we knew of this action was what we read in the newspapers Apprised in this blunt way, we did all we could to effect a change in policy by the authorities. Five different efforts were made by us to effect a change in policy, but to no avail Father Lee is on record that 'the most regrettable action by the state in his 32 years of pastorate here is the closing of the state police barracks in Salisbury' He personally told the representatives of the state police, who called at St. Joseph's rectory three weeks ago in regard to this matter that he knew Salisbury by 75 years of contact, as a native of Haverhill and pastor here, that he deplored the closing of the state police barracks

"The season is over now We all regret the mistake of the state police administration My reason for talking on it today is to clear your minds of any responsibility on our part for conniving at it More important—we urge you to write your pleas to the commissioner of state police, or to the governor, that this policy of a closed barracks of state police at Salisbury be not repeated next year We want the state police resident here, as they were for the past 10 years"

CLOSING OF STATE POLICE BARRACKS AT BEACH IS DEPLORED

Rev. Daniel F. Donovan Tells Auditors He "Regrets Mistake of Administration"— Urges Plea Against Repetition Next Year

At three masses Sunday in the Star of the Sea chapel at Salisbury Beach, Rev. Daniel F. Donovan, administrator of the St. Joseph's parish of Amesbury, deplored the closing this year of the state police barracks at the beach.

He said

"The moral issues at stake in the closing of the state police barracks here in Salisbury this summer are too grave to be ignored by your priests. Father Lee and I regret exceedingly this action. Lest any of you think that we were not interested in this matter, and that we did not make every effort to have the barracks reopened, I deem it necessary [...] questions to you.

"First of all, we agree with most of you who have given this matter any thought that there is urgent need here of resident state police Salisbury Beach is the only summer resort on the entire coast of this state with a large-scale amusement paraphernalia that has not state or metropolitan police to supplement the regular local force during the season

when the population multiplies by 10 times the number of year-round residents, and where the nightly excursionists from nearby cities and towns increase by hundreds, and sometimes thousands, those who must be policed No other local force is obliged to care, practically alone, for such an increment of human beings especially where there are such amusement and liquor provisions. As far as I can find out, our local police are doing their duty as well as can be humanly expected But the problem is too big for them, as it would be for any similar force in the same circumstances The two state police officers, assigned from the Topsfield barracks—20 miles away—are doing their best also, but they are not here every night, nor can they cover the whole beach area, when they are here, according to the terms of the contract that the state made at the time that the Commonwealth took over the policing of the beach area 10 years ago.

"Secondly, the summer just ending may not have produced any murders or headline scandals, but it has not been one to make a resident proud of

(Continued on Page Five)

The Salisbury Beach Fire Control Tower can be seen on the beach in the upper right corner, taken ca. 1948. It is the only cottage actually on the beach.

Government photo of 155mm guns on Salisbury Beach.

This buried concrete Panama mount was uncovered in a 2013 storm.

Children playing in a Jeep at the Beach Tower, ca. 1945.

Blake in Charge Of Barracks at Salisbury Beach

State Trooper John C Blake lately of the Wrent' barracks is in charge of the Salisbury Beach summer barracks of the state police The summer sub station opened this week and has a force of six officers who will work not on at Salisbury Beach but in the district

With Trooper Blake who previously has been in charge there, are Troopers Julian T Zuk and George F Houghton of Topsfield barracks, Carl Larson of Wrentham barracks, Daniel Driscoll of Monson barracks and Walter Lashoto of Framingham barracks

The Salisbury Beach sub station is located a short distance north of the recreational area in a building constructed in wartime for the use of the Coast Guard There has been no summer barracks of the state police at Salisbury Beach since the war made the force shorthanded

In 1946, the state police began using the abandoned military observation post located directly on the beach. The 1946 Salisbury Beach detail consisted of the following personnel pictured above, Front, L to R: Trooper Daniel F. Driscoll, John C. Blake, Julian Zuk. Rear, L to R: George F. Houghton, Carl M. Larson and Walter D. LaShoto. Blake, Larson and Zuk all rose to the rank of Lt. Colonel, Houghton and Driscoll both retired with the rank of Captain, and LaShoto retired as a Sergeant.

ceased using the property and it was leased by the Commonwealth as a summer barracks for the Massachusetts State Police from 1946 through 1950. After flooding problems during high tides in 1950, the state police stopped renting the property. The cottage and concrete tower was toppled and destroyed in an April 1958 storm.

A temporary battery of four 155 mm guns on tractor drawn carriages was emplaced on "Panama Mounts" at Salisbury Beach State Reservation, completed in 1942. This battery was under the umbrella of the Boston Harbor Defense Command and was manned by Battery "B", 241st Coast Artillery Regiment (Harbor Defense) Massachusetts National Guard beginning in September 1941. A barracks, mess hall, HQ building and latrine were built behind the gun position on the reservation. Other than the remains of the Panama mounts, there are no visible remains of any military structures. Pictured on the previous page, the buried concrete Panama mount was uncovered in a 2013 storm and children playing in jeep at Beach Tower C.1945.

On August 15, 1943, a family staying in the Hale Cottage at 352 North End Boulevard Salisbury Beach reported that,

"…just after dinner the army truck began to come with all kinds of equipment, search lights, generators to furnish power for the lights and many other things that we did not know what they were for. A little later, while sitting on our piazza, military planes flying low and towing targets out over the ocean and along the coast came into sight and once they were in sight of the anti-aircraft batteries they would open fire and we could hear the burst of shells and see the target blasted from its tow line."

It must have been quite a spectacle for the summer residents of Salisbury Beach!

The 1947 Salisbury Beach detail consisted of the following personnel: Trooper Robert J. Mitchell OIC, Troopers John T. Sadler, Francis X. Barry, Paul A. Peterson, William J. Sullivan and Thomas D. Murphy. Thomas Murphy retired as a Lt. Colonel, Robert Mitchell and John Sadler retired as Captains, Francis Barry and William Sullivan as Lieutenants and Paul Peterson as a Trooper in 1960.

The 1948 Salisbury Beach detail consisted of the following personnel: Corporal Robert F. Bourbeau, Trooper Stephen S. Wersoski, Peter Zuk, Thomas Murphy, John Kulik and William Kane. Stephen Wersoski and Kane both retired as Staff Sergeants and Kulick as a Captain.

Robert J. Mitchell, 23rd RTT, 1930.   *Francis X. Barry, 32nd RTT, 1947.*   *William J. Sullivan, 26th RTT, 1934.*

Thomas D. Murphy, 29th RTT, 1941.   *John T. Sadler, 29th RTT, 1941.*   *Paul A. Peterson, 32nd RTT, 1947.*

William Kane, 32nd RTT, 1947.   *Captain Peter Zuk, 29th RTT, 1941.*   *Stephen S. Wersoski, 26th RTT, 1934.*

1945 Chevy Cruiser

The 1949 Salisbury Beach detail pictured above standing on the steps of the WWII cottage/tower build by US Government are, Left Bottom to Top: George C. Edwards, Hector J. Cote, Carl Larson. Right Bottom to Top: Alfred Hewitt, Walter Kornachuck and Paul Peterson. Alfred Hewitt was struck and killed while on duty on Route One in Lynnfield in 1950. George Edwards retired as a Sergeant in 1951, Hector Cote in 1968 as a Lieutenant, Carl Larson as Lt. Colonel in 1964, and Paul Peterson and Walter Kornachuck both retired as Troopers.

State Police Barracks At Salisbury Closed

The summer barracks of the state police at Salisbury Beach has closed, now that activity at the resort has been reduced with the passing of Labor day. During their stay at the beach the troopers did much police work, which included handling heavy week end and holiday traffic in the area, and co-operating with the Salisbury police.

Cpl. Robert F Bourbeau, in charge, returns to Framingham barracks Troopers Stephen S. Wersoski and Peter Zuk went to Topsfield barracks, Trooper Thomas Murphy and John J. Kulik to Andover and Trooper William Kane to Concord

Round Up Seven In Bookie Raids

Men Nabbed By State Police At Beach Resort; Cases Coming Up In Amesbury Court Friday

Cases of seven men, rounded up Saturday in connection with alleged bookie activities at Salisbury Beach were today continued by the Amesbury district court until Friday, at the request of state police.

On Saturday state police, in charge of Sgt. John C. Blake, of Troop A headquarters, Framingham, with eight troopers; Sgt. George C. Edwards of Salisbury Beach and Police Chief Charles Goodridge, rounded up six men at the beach and later in the evening, another man was picked up at Georgetown—Leo J. Riley, 39, of 23 Middle street, by Corporal Bourbeau and Trooper Swanson, on a warrant, with the charge registering horse bets.

Riley is a former state police sergeant, who was special investigator for State Atty. General Bushnell's office and more recently has been a Massachusetts private detective.

Others arrested were Paul Pattavina, 52, of 11 Central avenue, Salisbury Beach, charged with registering horse bets; Edward Foote, 37, of 18 North End boulevard, Salisbury Beach, same charge; William Papoulias, 29, of 7 Mudnock road, Salisbury, also on the same charge; Charles L. Papoulias, 23, of 7 Mudnock road, Salisbury, charged with allowing premises to be used for registering bets; Howard C. Stevens, 38, of 13 Shea street, Salisbury Beach, charged with registering bets and William E. Murray, Jr., 17, of 205 Elm street, Amesbury, both charged with being present where gambling implements were found.

Pattavina was arrested as he was leaving his home, about 3:45; Foote in an alley, between Broadway and Driftway about 3; William Papoulias near the premises of the Papoulias taxi cab office; Charles Papoulias, Murray and Stevens, also at or near the taxi cab premises.

Police Break Up 'Burley' Show

Four Men And Eight Women Arrested At Beach By State Police Squad—Cases Continued

A large squad of state police broke up a burlesque show in a tent at Central avenue and Driftway, Salisbury Beach, early today, arresting four men and eight women. In Amesbury district court this forenoon their cases were continued to Friday by agreement.

One man was charged with presenting an immoral show and the other men and all the women were charged with taking part in one. Two of the girls were described as "strip teasers" and the others as chorus girls

300 On Hand

An audience of 250 to 300 was in the tent. State police said that many young persons were in the audience. There was no panic because the police worked so efficiently they completed much of their work before the crowd caught on. One of the "strippers" at nearing the high spot of her act, which was to have been followed by the finale, when the troopers staged the impromptu finale.

The tent show had given its first performance Wednesday night. The show which was broken up was the midnight performance.

One of the so-called strippers, Dorothy Beath, is said to be known professionally as Lynn Page. The other alleged stripper, Isabel McDonald, is known on the stage as Rusty Blaine. All of the arrested persons hail from Boston and places nearby.

Joseph H Sarino, 29, 5 Fisk terrace, Allston, the alleged manager, was charged with presenting an immoral show. The other arrested persons all were booked for participating in an immoral show.

They are Sterling L. Beath, 34, 41 Gore street, Boston, said to be a comedian, Charles Robinson, 42, 21 Fayette street, Salisbury, and Peter J Floherty, 26, 24 Allston street, Boston, the ticket seller.

Audrey Ings, 20, of West Elm avenue, Wollaston, Doris Wilson, 29, 382 Beach street, Revere, Dorothy Beath, 26 41 Gore street, Boston; Mary D. Santry, 24, 150 L street, Boston.

Ann Kalis, 27, 82 Wilson street, Boston, Emily E. Dechrastopher, 24, 4581 Washington street, Boston; Isabel McDonald, 23, 7 Allen road, Boston; Louise B Surman, 24, of Walnut street, Revere

An audience of 250 to 300 was in the tent. State police said that many young persons were in the audience. The raid was made by the police staged their part of the show at 1:15 a m after having had observers in the audience. A couple of the girls were described as strippers and the others as chorus girls.

The police party was in charge of Sgt. Arthur F Chaisson of Framingham troop headquarters and State Policewoman Mary Kirkpatrick. Acting Cpl George C Edwards of Salisbury Beach barracks was with the raiders along with Troopers Carl Larson, Paul A Peterson and Alfred Hewitt, of Salisbury Beach barracks; Joseph O'Neil, William Grady and George Canty.

Chief Charles S. Goodridge of Salisbury was with the party

Fowler Is Graduated At Submarine School

Herbert N. Fowler, seaman apprentice, USN, son of Mr. and Mrs. Alvin J Fowler of 3 Gardner street, Salisbury, was recently graduated from the Enlisted Basic Submarine school, New London, Conn.

Show Manager And 13 Others Appeal Fines

Beach Cases Heard In Amesbury Court

AMESBURY—Thirteen defendants were found guilty of participating in an immoral show, by Judge Martin P Connelly in Second District court yesterday, and a 14th defendant was found guilty of managing an immoral show All were released after posting bonds.

The case arose from a state police raid early Saturday morning, July 2, at a burlesque show being presented in a large tent at the corner of the Driftway and Central avenue at Salisbury Beach

Nine Fined $15 Each

Those found guilty of participating in an immoral show were Ann Kalis, 27, 82 Wilson street, Boston; Andrey M. Ings, 20, West Elm avenue, Wollaston, Mary B. Santry, 24, 150 L street, South Boston; Emily E. Dechrastopher, 24, 4851 Washington street, Boston; Louise B Schuman, 34 Walnut street, Revere, Doris A. Wilson, 29, 382 Beach street, Revere, Dorothy Beath, 26, 41 Gore street, Boston.

Cafe Manager Appeals Fines

AMESBURY— Mario J Lucchesi of Railroad avenue, Salisbury Beach, manager of Jenny's cafe, appeared in Second District court here this morning before Judge Connelly on charges involving the running of an entertainment on Sunday without a license and permitting a minor to work in his establishment

On the first count he was fined $25, and on the second, $15 Lucchesi, who pleaded not guilty on both decisions He was released on $100 bond

Jenny's Cafe Inc. 28 Railroad avenue Salisbury Beach was found not guilty on two similar charges

The first witness for the prosecution was State Trooper George Edwards of the Topsfield barracks, formerly acting corporal of the Salisbury Beach barracks, who said he entered Jenny's cafe on Sunday afternoon, Sept 4 when a show was in progress.

The trooper testified that he asked Mr Lucchesi to produce his Sunday license and the manager replied that, while it was an oversight because he customarily had one, he did not have a license for that week He did Mr Edwards said that he then asked the age of a girl in the chorus line He was told she was Miss Corrine (Novak) Lavins, 20 of Boston Mr Lucchesi said this was not his responsibility as all shows are sent to his establishment through a Boston agency

Barracks At Salisbury To Be Opened Friday

The Salisbury Beach summer barracks of the state police at Salisbury Beach will open Friday. Inquiry of Lt. Arthur T. O'Leary, public relations officer for the state police, disclosed that Patrolman George C. Edwards, now stationed at Topsfield, will be detailed to take charge of the summer barracks.

Trooper Edwards, a resident of Haverhill, is an experienced officer and has served at Salisbury Beach. During the wartime and afterward he was in the naval service and did a great deal of investigative work.

The summer barracks will have about six men and they will work in co-operation with the police of the communities in the northeastern corner of the Bay State. The state police building is the structure on the seashore immediately north of the skating rink. It was put up in wartime for the U. S. Coast Guard.

1940 Ford Cruiser. The State Police began painting cruisers in French & Electric Blue in 1939.

THE FIFTIES

The 1950 Salisbury Beach detail consisted of the following personnel pictured below. Seated L to R: Trooper Carl Larson, 29th RTT; George C. Edward, 22nd RTT; Thomas Peterson, 33rd RTT. Standing L to R: Dan Desmond, 31st RTT; Joe Kelley, 34th RTT; Sergeant Robert Murgia, 33rd RTT; and Bronius Uzdawinis, 33rd RTT.

Edwards, in May 1942, shot and killed a suspect who had just murdered Trooper Charles Collins during a gun battle in Byfield. Trooper Peterson, along with Trooper Robert A. Long in 1970, captured Lefty Gilday, who was wanted for the murder of Boston Patrolman Walter A. Schroeder. This photo was taken inside the World War II lookout station that was built directly on the beach. Sergeant Murgia, who later became Lt. Colonel, related in an interview that a wild August storm washed right through the first floor of the barracks. After the 1950 storm, the state police relocated to a different location at 451 North End Boulevard. The World War II station was destroyed during a fierce ocean storm in April 1958 and toppled into the sea.

—WEDNESDAY, JUNE 21, 1950

FR. (AP)

State Police Detail Established at Salisbury Beach for Season

The Summer State Police Barracks has opened at Salisbury Beach, Commissioner of Public Safety John F. Stokes announced yesterday.

The station, which will remain open until after Labor Day, will cover the area north of the Newburyport Bridge to the New Hampshire line, formerly covered by the Topsfield Barracks.

The following officers will be on duty at the barracks: Trooper George C. Edwards in charge, assisted by Troopers Carl M. Larson, Daniel J. Desmond, John J. Kulik, Thomas H. Peterson, Joseph A. Kelly, and Bronius M. Uzdawinis, all members of Troop A.

William Grundy, who retired as a Captain.

John J. LaPoint, who retired as a Staff Sergeant.

In 1951, the State Police Salisbury Detail moved to a rented cottage at 541 North End Boulevard, Route 1A. The rent for the first year was $900 for the entire summer, Memorial Day through Labor Day. The barracks/cottage had an outside shower. Senior Trooper William Grady was the OIC, and Troopers Francis X. Barry, Thomas Peterson, George Houghton, Hector Cote, John J. Hyde and Maurice Foley were assigned. Grady and Houghton retired as Captains, John Hyde as a Major.

The 1952 Salisbury Beach detail consisted of the following personnel: Corporal John Downey, Troopers Joseph Sullivan, George Houghton, John LaPoint, Robert Murgia, Martin A. Murphy, and Edward Kelly.

Beach Troopers Staff Sergeant James Donahue and John Downy with President John F. Kennedy.

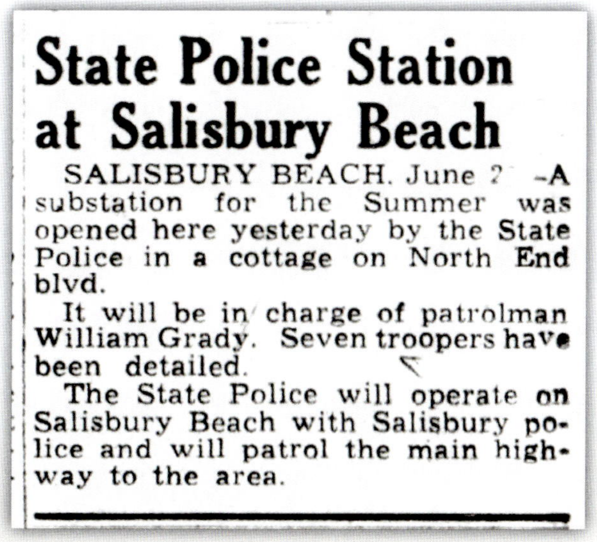

State Police Station at Salisbury Beach

SALISBURY BEACH. June ? —A substation for the Summer was opened here yesterday by the State Police in a cottage on North End blvd.

It will be in charge of patrolman William Grady. Seven troopers have been detailed.

The State Police will operate on Salisbury Beach with Salisbury police and will patrol the main highway to the area.

Arthur Jowett using the outside shower at the beach cottage/barracks.

In 1951, the State Police moved to this cottage at 541 North End Boulevard close to the New Hampshire state line.

Philip Mortimer, 34th RTT, 1948.

James Donahue, 31st RTT, 1947.

Maurice Foley, 35th RTT, 1949.

1953 Detail, Front L to R: James Donahue, Martin A. Murphy, Maurice Foley. Rear L to R: Philip Mortimer, Robert Herzog, George Houghton OIC. Missing from the photo is Bohdan W. Boluch. Boluch met and married his future wife, Ruth Olive Williams, while stationed at Salisbury Beach in 1953.

Hector Cote, 31st RTT, 1947.

Martin Murphy, 35th RTT, 1949.

John J. Murphy, 34th RTT, 1948.

Jerry Crowley, 36th RTT, 1952.

Sydney Scarth,
36th RTT, 1959.

Bohdan Boluch,
32nd RTT, 1947.

SALISBURY — State police personnel will use a two story wooden frame cottage on North End Boulevard at Salisbury Beach as temporary barracks for the summer months -the Governor's Council having approved lease of the property from May 15 to September 15 at a rental of $1,000 payable to John Stoyanoglu...The same facilities have been used in the past summers at a rental of $900, but it was explained the owner has redecorated the interior.

Claim Boys Took Bathers' Pocketbooks

The vigilance of a state trooper and a State Beach officer has resulted in the capture of five juvenile-age boys who allegedly have been stealing property of visitors at the Salisbury Beach state reservation.

Three of the boys, 9, 11, and 13 came before a juvenile session of the Amesbury district court this morning. State Trooper Leo Carney of the Salisbury Beach barracks and State Beach Officer Joseph A Wrigley apprehended the trio after identifying them as having stolen seven pocketbooks left on the beach

The contents of the pocketbooks are valued at nearly $200 The boys also took watches, it was alleged

It was claimed the young offenders executed their coup by dropping large Turkish towels over property left on the sand, and picking up the articles along with the towels

The two boys, apprehended last Saturday, lifted a pair of slacks belonging to a Somerville man, it was learned from the officers

Congdon Toll Road Closed, Says Judge

LAWRENCE, Oct. 14—Judge Paul G. Kirk said this about the "Congdon Toll Road" and the Salisbury Police Department in Superior Court today.

"Someone has been operating a private toll road in this Commonwealth. By your decision the Congdon toll road has been closed for good and I want to add that the Salisbury Police Department is an unmitigated disgrace."

Judge Kirk was addressing the jury which had found Congdon guilty. He thanked the panel for its services.

The 1954 Salisbury Beach detail consisted of the following personnel: Corporal Hector Cote, James M. Donahue, Edward Kelly, Joseph Kelley, John J. Murphy, Robert Herzog, and Martin A. Murphy.

The 1955 Salisbury Beach detail consisted of the following personnel: Corporal Hector Cote, Eugene Murphy, Joseph Kelley, Philip Mortimer, Leo Carney, John J. Murphy, and Maurice Foley.

The 1956 Salisbury Beach detail consisted of the following personnel pictured below: Corporal Robert D. Murgia, Jerry Crowley, Charles Gilligan, Joseph Kelley, Eugene Murphy, Donald MacDonald, Harry Reddish and Richard J. Crowley. Murgia retired as Lt. Colonel in 1972 after losing a suit against the forced retirement at age 50, Charles Gilligan also retired as a Lt. Colonel, MacDonald and Reddish as Captains, and both Crowley's as Corporals. In 1959, Gene Murphy took a leave of absence and was appointed the Chief of Police in Salisbury. He returned after the first year, as the Commissioner of Public Safety would not extend his leave, and he retired in 1968.

The 1957 Salisbury Beach detail consisted of the following personnel in the photo on the right: Seated L to R: Charles W. Gilligan, Sergeant Robert D. Murgia, Corporal Peter J. Murphy. Standing L to R: Troopers Robert J. Birmingham, Dominic Arena and Donald H. MacDonald. Missing when the photo was taken was Trooper William Irving. Arena left the state police in 1967 and took the position of Chief of Police in Edgartown, MA. He was the chief on July 18, 1969 when Senator Ted Kennedy drove his car off the Dike Bridge on Chappaquiddick Island, killing Mary Joe Kopechne. Robert Birmingham retired as a Sergeant in 1978 and Peter Murphy retired as a Lieutenant in 1972. Gilligan retired as a Lt. Colonel and Murgia retired as a Lt. Colonel/Executive Officer.

In 1958, the detail consisted of Corporal George Wall, Lawrence Harding, Al Sabanski, John R. O'Donovan, Robert C. Woodward, and Eugene Murphy.

1959 Detail — among those assigned were: Sergeant John Kulik, Daniel Driscoll, Sid Scarth, John R. O'Donovan, William Stewart, Arthur Ober and Edward Mulligan. William Stewart and Arthur Ober retired as Staff Sergeants, Edward Mulligan and John Kulik retired as Captains, Sid Scarth and Dan Driscoll retired as Lieutenants.

Retired Major Richard Loynd, who worked for Sergeant John Kulik at Salisbury Beach, said of Sergeant Kulik, "He ruled it with an iron fist because otherwise.... all hell would break loose...(at the beach)."

Tipsy Driver Traveled at 90, State Trooper Informs Court

AMESBURY — An East Boston driver who was clocked at 90 miles per hour on the expressway in Amesbury yesterday, paid $60 in fines this morning in second district court before Judge Martin F. Connelly

Lyman F. Richard Jr. 249 Emerson street East Boston, was fined $50 for operating under the influence and another $10 for speeding

A companion Eddie J. Barnes, San Francisco, Calif, paid a $15 fine for allowing an improper person to operate his car

State Trooper Dominic Arena of Salisbury barracks told the court that the defendant was driving on the Californian's license

by Trooper Arena who was also the complainant in the case of Maurice P Licciardi, 33 Bruce street, Lawrence, who paid $10 for left of way driving in Salisbury, also on July 2

Boston Street To Be Fixed

NEWBURY — Selectmen Silas Little and Martin H Burns went to the State Department of Public Works office in Danvers yesterday seeking advice on Boston Street reconstruction. At the annual town meeting last March the town appropriated $2,500 to improve the sec-

Salisbury Barracks Report of Action

SALISBURY — Harry L Bagley, 26, of Folly Mill road, Smithtown was arrested by Sgt. Robert Murgia of the state police last night for operating after his right to had been suspended He was bailed for appearance in Amesbury court

Ernest G Dewhurst 31, 165 State street Newburyport was arrested at 8 last night by Trooper Irving for operating with a license in his possesion and after suspension of his license and also for speeding He also was bailed in $100 for appearance in Amesbury.

Wayne D Morgan 18 Fort Devens was arrested by state trooper Charles Gilligan for speeding at 8 30 last night

William W Miller 42 a vacationer on Old County road whose address is 59 Beach street Haverhill was arrested by Irving and Gilligan for drunkenness Police also report that a warrant has been issued by his wife for assault and battery He will appear in Amesbury court

Salisbury Beach Show Raided

SALISBURY — State Police revised the old saying "the show must go on" by stopping it in a raid at a aid at a Salisbury Beach night club last night.

The troopers, including a state police woman, stopped the act of an exotic dancer from Somerville and brought the house down.

Winifred R. Fountas, 19, of Melvin St., was charged with participating in an immoral show. George T. Hattar, 39, of Jackman St., Methuen, proprietor of The Barn was charged with staging such a show.

The pair were released in $200 bail each for a Sept. 15 appearance in Amesbury District Court.

The raiding party was headed by Trooper Albert Sabansky of the Foxboro Barracks. The police woman was Evelyn Kenney of the Northampton Barracks.

Corporal George Wall leading Troopers into a riot at Walpole State Prison.

GOING—GOING—GONE is this large structure at Salisbury Beach, formerly the home of the State Police. The rushing surf pounded the building and finally undermined it shortly before 10 o'clock this morning. The picture above was taken as the building started to fall into the sea. To the right is the same building immediately after. Debris was battering the shoreline, threatening many other buildings along the Salisbury coast line.

Savage Surf, High
Two-Story House Toppled Into Surf at Salisbury Beach

A 1958 storm topples MSP barracks into the sea.

Albert Sabanski, 36th RTT, 1952.

John Kulick, 33rd RTT, 1958.

Frank Mahoney, 38th RTT 1954.

Joseph W. Sullivan, 31st RTT 1947.

Staff Sergeant Arthur Ober.

Donald D. Callahan, 35th RTT 1949.

1956 Ford and Trooper Arthur Ober.

1959 Ford 2-door hardtop.

Arthur Ober, 39th RTT, 1956.

William Stewart, 39th RTT, 1956.

Carl J. Vets, 39th RTT, 1964.

Basil Walsh, 38th RTT, 1954

Captain R. Bourbeau with Fidel Castro and Trooper Stan Jackson at Logan Airport, 1959.

Maurice Foley and Ed Kelley, both beach troopers.

Refused To Leave Water

Gardner B Sargent, 30, 106 East Main street, Merrimac, was fined $5 for failing to heed the reasonable request of a lifeguard at Salisbury Beach He was arrested yesterday afternoon by Trooper Kelley when he refused to leave the water at the request of lifeguards.

Four Seabrook, N H. men were fined $10 each on charges of drunkenness as a result of a disturbance at Brown's park, Salisbury, last night The defendants were Chester F Downs 37, Frank P Chase. 50, Thomas F Owen Jr., 30, and Rodney N. Souther. 28 They were arrested by Cpl John F. Downey.

'Port Man Fined; For Drunk Driving

AMESBURY—Ivan Q. Eaton, 22, of 11 1-2 Marlboro street, Newburyport, paid a $35 fine for drunken driving following a hearing this morning before Judge Martin F. Connelly in second district court.

State Trooper Leo J. Carney, of the Salisbury Beach barracks, told the court that he stopped the defendant's car in Seabrook, N. H., July 19, after following it along Route 1-A, the north shore boulebard in Salisbury Beach.

Defaulted Driver Is Caught Again; Jailed for 10 Days

Ernest C Cramp. 21, of Lincoln, Maine was sentenced to 10 days in the house of correction Tuesday by Judge Norman Espovich in district court

Cramp had pleaded guilty to a charge of second offense of driving after the revocation of his license. The complaint was made by State Trooper Edward Mulligan of Salisbury Beach barracks

Court records showed that March 16 he was convicted of a first offense in Haverhill and was fined $75, suspended to March 21 He did not pay the fine and was declared defaulted

If the customary procedure is carried out, Haverhill police will take him on a warrant on his release after the 10-day sentence is served

Richard P. Hiller, 47th RTT, 1966.

William H. Irving (right) was a Beach Trooper in 1957.

Lt. Colonel Blake with President John F. Kennedy.

Larry Harding and Anthony Grillo

25

THE SIXTIES

The 1960 Salisbury Beach detail consisted of the following personnel: Sergeant John Kulik, Troopers Richard Schneiderhan, John R. O'Donovan, Armand Longval, Richard Loynd, James Oteri, John J. O'Donnell, and Richard Powers.

The 1961 Salisbury Beach detail consisted of the following personnel: Sergeant John Kulick, Troopers John R. O'Donovan, Richard Loynd, Richard Schneiderhan, Armand Longval, James V. Oteri, Anthony Grillo, Thomas Cain, Richard Powers, and George Strout.

TROOPERS MOVE TO BEACH

State police yesterday announced their summer station at Salisbury Beach will open today. Sgt. John J. Kulik will be in charge.

George Strout, 32nd RTT, 1947.

James Oteri in uniform, 37th RTT, 1953.

Richard Loynd, 41st RTT, 1957.

2 Cops Hurt in Salisbury Brawl

SALISBURY — Two state troopers were brutally beaten today when they were jumped by a mob as they attempted to arrest a man who authorities said, has caused a disturbance in Shannon's Inn, a dine and dance spot on Lafayette rd.

Three men, said by police to have been members of the mob, were grabbed by reinforcements who were rushed to the scene when troopers Richard N.

Loynd, 26, and John R. O'Donovan, 30, of the Salisbury Beach substation were overpowered.

Taken into custody on a variety of charges, including inciting a riot, attempting to rescue a prisoner, and assault and battery on a police officer, were Wilfred P. Welch, 21, Gardner st., and Arnold W. Bishop, 21, of North End blvd., both Salisbury, and Bert (Beano) Abrahams, 25, of South

Main st., Seabrook, N. H.

Loynd and O'Donovan were removed to Anna Jaques Hospital, Newburyport, where they were placed under observation for possible concussion.

According to police, the brawl erupted shortly after midnight when the two troopers went to the inn on the report of a disturbance, and took a man, thus far unidentified, into custody.

As they were leaving, authori-

ties said, a gang of several men closed in, and began slugging them. Loynd and O'Donovan, attempting to prevent their prisoner from escaping, were knocked to the floor where, police said, some of the mob held them while the rest kicked them about the head and body.

A call for help was made to the Salisbury police and to the state police barracks at Lynnfield and Topsfield, and, within

a few minutes, reinforcements arrived at the scene.

They managed to rescue Loynd and O'Donovan and arrest Welch, Bishop, and Abrahams. All three were booked and held at the poical police station until they were taken to court.

The prisoner, over whom the brawl exploded, managed to escape in the uproar, police said, but he was reported to have been rearrested later.

Donald MacDonald, Thomas Cain, and John O'Donovan, all Beach Troopers.

Richard Loynd

Trooper Richard Barry 40th RTT, 1956 , with President John F. Kennedy and Arthur M. Schlesinger, 1961.

James T. Canty,
41st RTT, 1957.

Vincent Caggiano and Donald MacDonald, 1962. Both of their wives had twins.

Heart Seizure Patient Aided By State Police

SALISBURY BEACH — Emergency first aid was given in a hurry by state troopers when a woman was brought to the barracks at 5 30 a m, suffering from an apparent heart attack which came on her in a Seabrook Beach cottage

The woman, Mrs ' Helen McKaig, 44, 144 Warren avenue, Chelmsford, was administered oxygen until it was safe to move her to the Anna Jaques hospital. Troopers Vincent Caggiano and Arthur Jowett took her to the hospital.

This forenoon the hospital reported Mrs McKaig to be resting comfortably.

The 1962 Salisbury Beach detail consisted of the following personnel: Corporal Peter Murphy OIC, Troopers Paul Beloff, Armand Longval, Carl Vets, Richard Barry, Donald MacDonald, Francis Mahoney, and Chester Hallice.

The 1963 Salisbury Beach detail consisted of the following personnel: Sergeant Peter Murphy, Troopers Vincent Caggiano, Arthur Jowett, Robert Birmingham, Charlie Coe, Cornelius Mike Linehan, Richard Lewis, Robert Keeler, Basil Walsh, and Donald MacDonald.

1964: Troopers began wearing the Campaign Hat in 1964. Rumor has it, there were many arrests of intoxicated vacationers for uttering, "Here comes Smokey The Bear."

Assigned to the beach detail were. Troopers Arthur Jowett, James Canty, Harry Boyd, Robert Sullivan, Cornelius Mike Linehan, Francis Leary, Donald Callahan, Anthony Grillo, Vincent Caggiano, and John Gilman.

1965: Sergeant Joseph Kelley OIC, Corporal James Killoran, Francis Leary,

Troopers Chester Hallice and Richard Powers testing future summer hats. Both were Beach Troopers in the 1960s.

John J. Cronin, Lawrence Fay, John Gilman, Cornelius Mike Linehan, Arthur J. Scott, Vincent Caggiano.

1966: Detail – Among those assigned were. Corporal Richard Loynd, Corporal Donald Callahan, Troopers Joseph Stone, Ken Dunphy, Vincent Caggiano, Michael Linehan, Robert Sullivan, Warren Bailey, Robert Kane, and William Cummings.

1967 Salisbury Beach Detail (pictured top right), Front: Warren Bailey and Kenneth Dunphy. Rear: Mike Noone, George Murphy, and Corporal Richard

20 Arrested In Salisbury Marijuana Raid

SALISBURY BEACH — Twenty men and women were arrested Saturday night in a narcotics raid on a North End blvd. cottage by State and Salisbury Police.

The raiding party was headed by Sgt. Richard Loynd of the Salisbury Beach State Police Summer barracks and Salisbury Chief Grant E. Morse and included two members of the State Police narcotics squad.

Police said a quantity of marijuana was seized. The raiders surrounded the cottage shortly before 10:30 p.m. making sure no one got away.

Those arrested were charged with being present where narcotics were kept.

N. Loynd. Not present for the photo were James Canty, John Gilman and Robert Sullivan. Warren Bailey and Mike Noone retired as Captains, George Murphy as a Corporal, Ken Dunphy as a Trooper and Dick Loynd as a Major.

1968 Detail – Among those stationed as the beach were Corporal Richard O'Neill, Corporal Arthur Jowett, Alfred Welcome, Bruce Latham, Robert Sullivan, Carmen Tammaro, Paul French, and Gerald Zundell.

1969 Detail – Among those stationed at the beach were Sergeant Arthur Jowett, Corporal Amie Blouin, Troopers John Murphy, Fred Johnston, Frank McVeigh, Bob Morrissey, Dick Hiller, Henry Sullivan, and Tom Dooling. Henry Sullivan retired as a lieutenant, Fred Johnston and Arthur Jowett retired as Staff Sergeants, Aime Blouin and John Murphy as Sergeants and Frank McVeigh, Bob Morrissey and Tom Dooling as Troopers. Arthur Jowett was a giant of a man and looked even bigger in uniform with the "Smokey The Bear Cover."

Four Rescued in 'Worst Riptide'

By ART JONES

SALISBURY — The water was unusually rough, but things were quiet on the waterfront yesterday until lifeguards were hit with successive rescue calls late in the afternoon

In what was described by one lifeguard as the "worst riptide I've seen in five years," four persons were rescued from rippling beach water by Salisbury lifeguards Sunday.

The first emergency came just before 5 p m when a 10-year old boy was caught in the rip His father dove in after him and both were being swept by the strong current.

Seven Rescuers — It took five guards and two State troopers to pull them free of the terrific current.

Guard Terry Kalil noticed the father and his son in the water and he notified nearby lifeguard posts and the first aid room He and Barry McCarthy were the first guards into the water.

Guards, Joe Kane, Bob Chouinard and Ed Foote also came to the rescue

McCarthy rescued the father from the waves and Kalil and Kane pulled the young lad out. Two troopers, wading in uniform helped man the lifeline which was used to haul them from the riptide.

Guard Paul Kelly came down from another post along with the first aid wagon to lend assistance.

The troopers were Sgt. Richard Loynd and Trooper Richard Hiller of the Salisbury Barracks The incident took place near the barracks on Northern Boulevard

Guards Jerry Grasso of Hav-
See FOUR on Page 10

Directory

Paul French,
48th RTT, 1967.

Charlie Coe,
39th RTT, 1956.

Aime Blouin with Bloodhound Sid.

Arthur Jowett at A-5 Salisbury.

Sergeant Martin Murphy with nephew Trooper Pat Fay and Father James Dunford, the first State Police Chaplain, and Martin's son Martin F. Murphy.

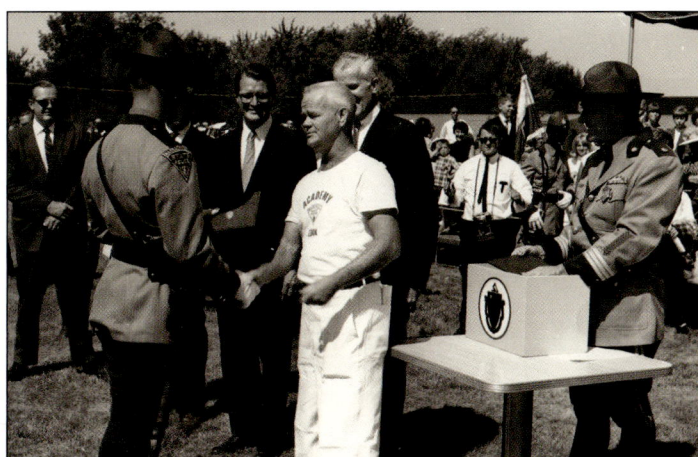

Trooper Frank McVeigh being Congratulated by his father Specky, long time Head Cook at the State Police Academy, 1966.

Harry Boyd, 37th RTT, 1953. Note the radio handset.

Trooper Joseph Stone in front of Willy's Jeep 4-wheel drive used at Salisbury Beach.

Richard Lewis,
42nd RTT, 1959.

Armand Longval,
36th RTT, 1952.

Carmen V. Tammaro,
48th RTT, 1967.

Cornelius Mike Linehan,
42nd RTT, 1959.

Paul Beloff, 41st RTT, 1957.

First troopers assigned to the new Leominster Barracks upon the closing of SP Shirley, Nov. 1957. First row: Cpl. W. St. Michael, Sgt. R. Ilg, Cpl. G. Nickerson. Second row: Tprs. F. Leary, A. Ritchie, W. Cummings. Third row: Tprs. R. Patterson, G. Scales, L. Thompson. Fourth row: Tprs. H. Boyd, R. Eithier, J. Killoran. Leary, Cummings, Boyd and Killoran were beach troopers in the 1960's.

Robert G. Sullivan being pinned by his father, Lieutenant William J. Sullivan. Both Sullivans served at the beach.

Lt. Colonel James Canty with Pope John Paul II. Superintendent Frank Trabucco is kissing the Pope's ring.

Ed Johnson and Bruce Latham, 1984. Bruce had a heart attack and died the day after this picture was taken.

1960 Ford Ranch Wagon.

Tom McNulty, 49th RTT, 1967.

Frederick L. Johnston, 48th RTT, 1967.

Ron Bellanti, 46th RTT, with Muhammad Ali at Logan Airport, 1964.

Chester E. Hallice Jr., 41st RTT 1957

Arthur J. Scott Jr., 45st RTT 1962

Frank J. McVeigh Jr., 47th RTT 1966

Henry E. Sullivan, 46th RTT 1964

Richard D. O'Neill, 37th RTT 1953

John Murphy, 52nd RTT 1968

Troopers Thomas M. Dooling and Richard P. Hiller both in the 47th RTT 1966 in front of Salisbury Substation A-5

Lieutenant Henry E. Sullivan (Retired) in front of Museum 1951 Ford

THE SEVENTIES

1970 Detail – Those assigned were Sergeant Arthur Jowett, Troopers Thomas Dooling, Thomas McNulty, Thomas Walsh, Ronald Bellanti.

On May 1, 1971, Commissioner William F. Powers, brought an end to the requirement that Troopers live in the Barracks. The 84 hour work was eliminated and replaced with a forty-hour work week and every officer issued a cruiser. A career incentive program was implemented (Quinn Bill), payment for court time was authorized and the department was reorganized. This meant that the state would no longer have to rent a summer station at Salisbury Beach. To supplement the need for troopers at the beach, patrols were sent from the Topsfield Barracks. But that did not work well. The beach was busier than ever, the Salisbury Beach State Reservation was growing in popularity and the use of drugs was on the increase. The beach was out of control and drunks and motorcycle groups were taking over the beach.

In 1973, Governor Francis Sargent signed legislation lowering the drinking age in Massachusetts from twenty-one to eighteen. Young people were killing themselves on the highways and drinking at Salisbury Beach was out of control. In 1975, Salisbury Police Chief Grant Morse, the Salisbury Board of Selectmen and Roger Shaheen, owner of Shaheen's Fun-O-Rama, requested that the state police detail be reinstituted. The chief provided office space in the Salisbury Police Station and a secretary for the troopers.

In 1975, the detail started up and those assigned are pictured below :Staff Sergeant John Cronin, Corporal John Gilman, Troopers Dan Twomey, Steve Gravelle, Roger Ford, Ed Desmond, Mike Mucci and Robert Morrissey. John Cronin

SALISBURY BEACH PATROL COMMENDED. State Troopers, from left, Cpl. John W. Gilman (in off-duty clothes), Stephen L. Gravelle, Michael C. Mucci, Roger A. Ford, Edward A. Desmond, Daniel J. Twomey, and S-Sgt. John J. Cronin are shown before leaving Salisbury Beach for winter assignments. Off-duty and not present when photo was taken was Trooper Robert D. Morrissey. Patrol was commended by Troop A Commander Capt. Frederick Henley of Framingham headquarters.

Pope John Paul II on a visit to Boston in 1979. Beach Trooper Michael Mucci is over the Pope's left shoulder behind the priest.

1978 Ford Cruiser

Captain John J. Cronin Jr., Troop "E".

President Ronald Reagan being greeted at Logan Airport by Troopers Tom Walsh, Jim Marshall, and Mike Mucci (third from right). Walsh and Mucci were Beach Troopers.

Robert J. Morrissey, 49th RTT, 1967.

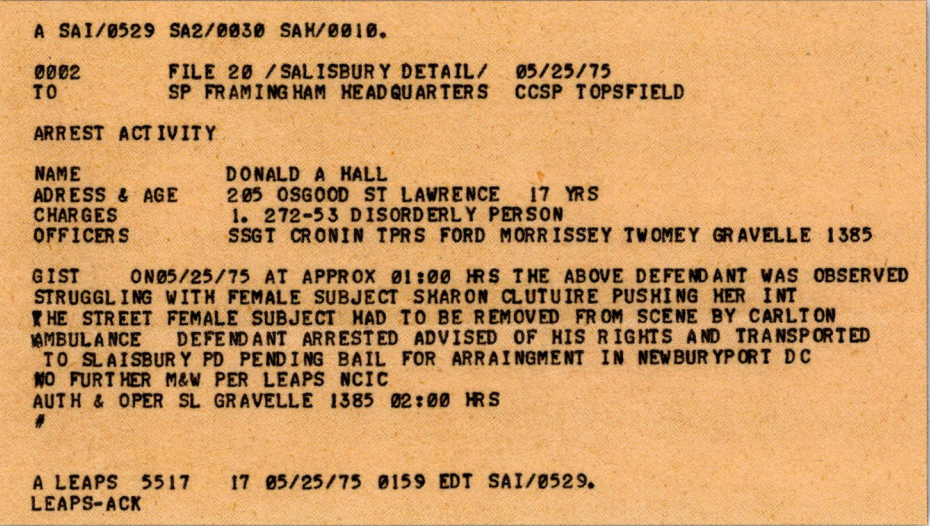

```
A SAI/0529 SA2/0030 SAH/0010.

0002        FILE 20 /SALISBURY DETAIL/  05/25/75
TO          SP FRAMINGHAM HEADQUARTERS  CCSP TOPSFIELD

ARREST ACTIVITY

NAME             DONALD A HALL
ADRESS & AGE     205 OSGOOD ST LAWRENCE  17 YRS
CHARGES          1. 272-53 DISORDERLY PERSON
OFFICERS         SSGT CRONIN TPRS FORD MORRISSEY TWOMEY GRAVELLE 1385

GIST     ON 05/25/75 AT APPROX 01:00 HRS THE ABOVE DEFENDANT WAS OBSERVED
STRUGGLING WITH FEMALE SUBJECT SHARON CLUTUIRE PUSHING HER INT
THE STREET FEMALE SUBJECT HAD TO BE REMOVED FROM SCENE BY CARLTON
AMBULANCE  DEFENDANT ARRESTED ADVISED OF HIS RIGHTS AND TRANSPORTED
TO SLAISBURY PD PENDING BAIL FOR ARRAIGNMENT IN NEWBURYPORT DC
NO FURTHER M&W PER LEAPS NCIC
AUTH & OPER SL GRAVELLE 1385 02:00 HRS
#

A LEAPS 5517  17 05/25/75 0159 EDT SAI/0529.
LEAPS-ACK
```

1975 Teletype message reporting the arrest of a disorderly person.

and John Gilman retired as Captains, Mike Mucci retired as Major, Steve Gravelle and Roger Ford as Lieutenants and Ed Desmond as a Trooper. The designation of Sub-Station A-5 was used from 1935 until barracks life end in 1970. When the detail started up again in 1975 the designation of Sub-Station A-6 was instituted.

1975 – Hell Angels The Bowery

One rainy evening while on foot patrol at Salisbury Beach, Troopers Robert Morrissey and Steve Gravelle were dispatched to the Bowery Night Club. The Bowery was featuring go-go dancers in cages above the dance floor and had become a problem establishment that the Troopers were well aware of. The owner of the club phoned the Salisbury Police and complained that a dozen Hells Angels in full colors had driven their motorcycles into the club and onto the dance floor to get out of the rain and refused to move them. Morrissey and Gravelle, both huge men well over six feet and both high school and college

football players, responded. Morrissey, according to Gravelle, waded into the center of the over-crowded club and ordered the Hells Angels to get on their motorcycles and get out of Salisbury. Without comment, the Angels got on their motorcycles and left Salisbury in the pouring rain.

1975 – Hells Angels Stabbing at the Bowery

On June 5, 1975 a Salisbury resident was stabbed in the back which punctured his lung as he entered The Bowery night club at Salisbury Beach. Troopers Robert Morrissey and Steven Gravelle, along with the Salisbury Police, responded. Two notorious members of the Hells Angels motorcycle gang were later arrested after they were identified in a photo lineup conducted by Trooper Gravelle. They were arraigned in Amesbury Court on the charge of assault with intent to murder and held in $50,000 bail each and were later indicted by a grand jury. The victim spent eighteen days in the hospital and made a full recovery.

1976 Detail, pictured below L to R: Troopers Roger Ford, Dan Grabowski, Dan Twomey, Ted Harvey, Steve Gravelle, Ed Desmond and Staff Sergeant Anthony Grillo. Roger Ford retired as a Lieutenant and joined the MBTA Police, Grabowski retired as a Major, Dan Twomey was elected President of SPAM, Ted Harvey and Steve Gravelle both retired as Lieutenants, Ed Desmond as a Trooper and Anthony Grillo as Colonel/Deputy Superintendent.

1977 – No Group Photo taken. Assigned to the Detail were: Troopers John Simpson, Edward Johnson, Mike Phair, Roger Ford, Dan Grabowski, Steve Gravelle, John O'Malley, Ron Guilmette, and Staff Sergeant Anthony Grillo. Ed Johnson dislocated his shoulder on the first weekend chasing a fleeing felon and was replaced by Jack O'Malley. John Simpson left the state police and had a career with the US Secret Service, Dean Bennett retired as a Lieutenant after serving as a helicopter pilot in the Air Wing, Dick DeLesDernier retired as a Trooper, Ed Johnson and Jack O'Malley both retired as detective lieutenants and Ron Guilmette as a Lt. Colonel and later served as Chief of Police in Lawrence and Chief of Police at Merrimack College.

State trooper injured while making arrest

SALISBURY — A state police officer was injured early Saturday morning while attempting to arrest a 24-year-old Woburn man.

Officer Edward Johnson suffered a dislocated shoulder in the struggle with Walter J. Pizzano, 45 Merrimac St., Woburn. Johnson was taken by Carleton Ambulance Service to Anna Jaques Hospital, Newburyport, where he was treated and released.

Pizzano was charged with assault and battery on a police officer, possession of fireworks, and disorderly conduct after his 1:25 a.m. arrest.

His bail, first set at $500, was later reduced to personal recognizance. He is scheduled to be arraigned in Amesbury District Court Monday morning.

Robert F. Monahan, 50th RTT, 1968.

Roger Calderwood, 59th RTT, 1974.

1978 Detail, pictured L to R: Troopers Dean Bennett, Richard DeLesDernier, Ron Guilmette, Steve O'Brien, John Simpson, Jack O'Malley, Charlie Tarsook and Sergeant Joe Roche. Charlie Tarsook retired as a Trooper, Steve O'Brien as a Lieutenant and Michael "Joe" Roche as a Major and worked at the Essex County Sheriff's Office for many years after retirement.

1979 Detail, pictured L to R: Troopers Steve O'Brien, Charlie Eastman, Dean Bennett, Dick DeLesDernier, Corporal Ron Guilmette, Jack O'Malley, John Simpson and Sergeant Bill Brooks. Charlie Eastman died of cancer while still serving as a Trooper in the Narcotics Unit and Bill Brooks retired as Sergeant.

THE EIGHTIES

1980 - Troopers Save Two

Two subjects, one a lifeguard and a teenage boy, were electrically shocked while in the water slide at Salisbury Beach. Trooper Steve Gravelle, while on time off, observed the two subjects get shocked and stop breathing. Gravelle had the power shut off at the site and immediately began CPR on one subject, who had turned blue. Sergeant Robert Mona-han, Corporal Ron Guilmette and Troopers Mike Ferrick and John Curtin responded and assisted with CPR on both subjects. Both were transported to Anna Jaques Hospital, with the Troopers continuing CPR in the Ambulance on the way to the hospital. Both subjects were admitted to intensive care and they both survived thanks to the quick action of Trooper Gravelle and assisting officers.

1980 Detail, pictured L to R: Troopers Dean Bennett, Michael Ferrick, James Young, John Curtin, Corporal Ron Guilmette and Sergeant Robert Monahan. Mike Ferrick, Jim Young and John Curtin retired as Troopers and Bob Monahan as a Lieutenant.

1981 Detail, pictured L to R: Troopers Richard Connelly, Thomas Donohue, Donald Kennefick, Thomas Robbins, Thomas Walsh, John Curtin, Sergeant Ron Guilmette and Sergeant Robert Monahan. Richard Connelly retired as a Sergeant, Tom Donohue as a Captain, Don Kennefick as a Detective Lieutenant, Tom Robbins as Colonel/Superintendent and Tom Walsh as Lt. Colonel/Deputy Superintendent.

1982 Detail, pictured L to R: Staff Sergeant Dick Downey, Troopers Tom Robbins, John Curtin, Don Kennefick, Tom Donohue, Steve Beaudoin, Richard Connelly, Sergeant Ron Guilmette. Dick Downey retired as a Captain and had a second career with the FAA Sky Marshalls and Steve Beaudoin retired as a Trooper.

Steve Gravelle and Ron Guilmette

Troopers conclude beach duty

SALISBURY — During the three months the State Police were at Salisbury Beach this summer they made 652 arrests. Two hundred-twenty drug related arrests included cocaine, herion and marijuana.

There were 13 arrests for operating under the influence of alcohol; six assault and battery on police officers; several arrests were made for possession of dangerous weapons which include sawed-off shot gun, sword, hand guns and nunchucks. Taken under protective custody, were 192 individuals.

Other arrests were: disorderly conduct, malicious damage to property, larceny, violation of town bylaws, public drinking and failure to move for police officers.

The state police arrived in Salisbury for Memorial Day and they completed their stay the Friday after Labor Day. Their work was primarily around the beach though they did some work at the state reservation. Their work day began at 6 pm. and patrolled until 2:30 a.m.

They still have court cases pending and these will continue with a back-up into December.

The officers had an office in the Salisbury Police

Station and the town furnished them a secretary, Michelle Champagne.

Sgt. Ronald J. Guilmette, second in charge of the troopers said it was a very busy summer but not as much so as last year. It was a productive summer, and more of a family element was noticed at the beach, he said.

The troopers said they wanted to thank Chief Edwin Oliveira and the entire police force for their cooperation, also the selectmen for requesting their stay at the beach and to the merchants for their cooperation.

Chief Oliveira in turn thanked the State Police officers for their assistance, as there are so many thousands of people at the beach during the summer, to whom the troopers provide much needed service.

The State Police who were stationed for the summer were: Sgt. Richard E. Downey who was in charge. Sgt. Guilmette, second in command; both are stationed at the Framingham Barracks. Trp. Thomas G. Robbins and Trp. Curtin John J. Curtin, and Trp. Stephen D. Beaudoin both of Topsfield; Trp. Thomas B. Donoghue, Andover, Trp. Richard P. Connelly, Foxboro.

Troopers Robbins and Connelly on Patrol with the Salisbury PD van.

1983 Detail, pictured L to R: Staff Sergeant Dick Downey, Troopers Steve Beaudoin, Tom Robbins, Steve Gravelle, Rob Smith, Don Kennefick, Richard Connelly, and Staff Sergeant Ron Guilmette. Rob Smith retired as Lieutenant in charge of the State Police Air Wing.

1984 Detail, pictured L to R: Staff Sergeant Ron Guilmette, Troopers Tom Robbins, Steve Beaudoin, Bob Krom, Steve Gravelle, Dennis Brooks, Don Kennefick, Tom Elias. Bob Krom, Dennis Brooks and Tom Elias all retired as Lieutenants.

1985 Detail, pictured L to R: Corporal Ed Johnson, Troopers George Chaisson, Paul Fletcher, Bob Krom, Dennis Brooks, Tom Coffey, Don Kennefick and Tom Elias. Paul Fletcher retired as a Lieutenant, Tom Coffey as a Detective Lieutenant and George Chaisson as a Sergeant.

1986 Detail, pictured L to R: Troopers Don Kennefick, Dennis Brooks, Rob Smith, Bob Krom, Staff Sergeant James Michael Toomey, Corporal Rod Hendrigan, Thomas Coffey and Tom Elias. James Twomey retired as a Captain and Rod Hendrigan retired as a Lieutenant.

1987 Detail, pictured L to R:
Troopers Don Kennefick, Dana
Pagley, Rob Smith, Bob Krom,
Staff Sergeant James Michael
Toomey, Kenny Gill, Al Manzi
and Tom Elias. Dana Pagley re-
tired as a Detective Lieutenant
and Kenny Gill retired as a Cap-
tain and Al Manzi retired as a
Trooper after almost 45 years of
service.

1988 Detail, pictured L to R:
Corporal Ed Connolly, Al Zani,
Don Kennefick, Bob Krom, Dana
Pagley, Al Manzi, Scott Pare and
Corporal Bob Laprel. Ed Connolly
and Al Zani retired as Lieutenants
and Scot Pare and Bob Laprel
both retired as Majors.

1989 Detail, pictured L to R: Corporal Tom Robbins, Troopers Steve Beaudoin,
David Rizos, Scott Pare, Al Manzi, Bob Krom and Sergeant Bob Laprel. Dave
Rizos retired as a Trooper.

1988 Police Cruiser

THE NINETIES

1990 Detail, pictured L to R: Sergeant Bob Laprel, Troopers David Rizos, Steve Alvino, Mike Cooney, Bob Krom, Ross Panacopoulos, Barry Brodette and Corporal Ed Horton. Barry Brodette and Ross Panacopoulos retired as a Sergeants, Ed Horton and Mike Cooney as Lieutenants.

1991 Detail, kneeling L to R: Corporal Scott Pare, Sergeant Bob Laprel, Corporal Craig Magner. Standing: Barry Brodette, Steve Alvino, Steve Beaudoin, Roger Calderwood, Al Manzi and Paul Perry. Craig Magner retired as a Sergeant, Steve Alvino and Roger Calderwood both retired as Troopers. Trooper Paul A. Perry was tragically killed in the line of duty while piloting a state police helicopter in Cambridge, Massachusetts on February 22, 1995. His Trooper co-pilot James Mattaliano and two civilian occupants were also killed. Paul was survived by his wife and two children.

1992 Detail, pictured L to R: Corporal George Credit, Troopers Al Manzi, Steve Alvino, Bob Krom, Joe Donlon, Ted Downer, Barry Brodette and Staff Sergeant Bob Laprel. George Credit retired as a Detective Lieutenant, Joe Donlon as a Sergeant and Ted Downer as a Lieutenant.

1993 Detail, pictured L to R: Sergeant Dennis Bertulli, Troopers Richard Eubanks, Roger Calderwood, Eddie Amodeo, Sergeant George Credit, Trooper Greg Ambrose, Joseph Donlon and Frank Devillis. Dennis Bertulli and Richard Eubanks retired as Sergeants, Roger Calderwood Joe Donlon and Frank Devillis as Troopers and Ed Amadeo as Lt Colonel.

1994 Salisbury Beach Summer Detail, standing L to R: Sergeant Dennis Bertulli, Troopers Richard Eubanks, Steve Alvino, Mike Currier, and Sergeant Dan Wicks. Kneeling: Trooper Thomas Canning, Kevin O'Neil, Peter Carbone and Ed Amadeo. Mike Currier and Peter Carbone retired as a Troopers, Dan Wicks retired as a Captain, Kevin O'Neil as a Sergeant and Eddie Amodeo as a Lt. Colonel.

1995 was the last year of the Salisbury Beach Detail. No group photo was taken. Assigned for the summer were: Sergeant Dan Wicks, Sergeant Jeff Dooling, Sergeant Robert Follett, and Troopers Brian Eng, Joseph Stone and Patrick Silva. Pat Silva retired as a Sergeant, Brian Eng retired as a Captain, and Joseph Stone retired as a Trooper. Stone's father was a Beach Trooper in 1966.

Patrick R. Silva, 72nd RTT, 1994

Brian T. Eng, 71st RTT, 1993

Joseph A. Stone Jr. 71st RTT, 1993

Epilogue

In 1933, the 18th Amendment, which illegalized the manufacturing, transportation and sale of alcohol, was abolished with the passage of the 21st Amendment. The Roaring Twenties was over. During the thirteen years that prohibition was in effect, Salisbury was a wide open port for rum-running and illegal operations. The Salisbury Police Chief, Harold Congdon, two selectmen, and two police officers had been imprisoned for rum running and leading a corrupt organized enterprise. Congdon also served as Chairman of the Board of Salisbury Selectmen during the same time he was chief and his wife, twin brother, and son served on the police department. If you were a friend of the chief, getting an appointment to the police department was a certainty. After he served his jail time, he was re-elected as a selectmen and appointed again to the police department, this time as a Captain. In 1956, he was convicted for posing as a state trooper and collecting cash fines from speeders on Route One, the Newburyport Turnpike. He was sent to jail a second time as Judge Paul Kirk, declared, "The Congdon Toll Road is now closed."

By the time the state police were assigned to Salisbury in 1933, it was a wide open community where anything went and the "Good Ole Boy Network" was in full swing.

In the forties, fifties and sixties, Salisbury Beach got the reputation of being "Honky-Tonk." The town actually voted to go dry for a year in 1956, but the following year it was voted back in. In 1959, a state trooper was appointed to serve as chief with a promise to clean up the town, but he returned to the state police after one-year because his leave of absence was not extended. The Boston gangland murders of the 1960s is said to have gotten its start in a nightclub at Salisbury Beach. Fights and drunkenness continued and the need for additional police presence grew.

In the sixties, seventies and eighties, the beach population grew and in the early 80s there was at least seventeen barrooms in the beach center, including; Mazie's Pink Elephant (later called Mr. K's) and then Mick & Matts, Butch & Joe's Club Royale, the Bowery (now the 10's Show Club), the Kon Tiki, the Tic Toc (later called Bevie B's), Normandy Lounge, Shaffie's, the Sands (now the Capri Restaurant), the Five O'clock Club (which was destroyed in the Blizzard of 1978 and replaced by the Ocean Club [now the Blue Ocean Event Center]), the Surf-Side 5 (built to replace the 5 O'clock which became the Surf-Side), the Sidewalk Café (where Eddie B. Baker played), the Peppermint Lounge (which burned down in 1977), Uncle Eddie's, the Carousel, the Dolphin, the Edwards Hotel, the Turf & Surf (where Sweet Pie performed on his piano with just a G-string) and the famous Frolics. The weekend crowds of 40,000 every weekend during the 1940s had more than doubled to 100,00 after two decades during summer weekends. Drug use was rampant. It was nothing for the seven troopers to arrest over 700 people every summer from 1977 through 1995.

In its heyday, the Frolics was the home of world class entertainment that featured performers such as Tony Bennett, Connie Francis, Paul Anka, Martha Raye, Mickey Rooney, Pat Boone, Louis Armstrong, Duke Ellington, Patti Page, Jimmy Dean, Johnny Mathis, Sammy Davis Jr., the Maguire Sisters, and many more. Ladies and gentlemen wore their best attire to attend an event at the Frolics. But, by the late sixties and early seventies they were hosting Big Time Wrestling, Mud Wrestling, Jell-O wrestling, boxing events, and local rock bands.

In 1975, the Roller Coaster was torn down, and in 1977 the famous "Salisbury Flying Horses" Carousel was sold and

Trooper David McCann on patrol, 2014.

Trooper Giuseppe Ciampa and visitor Kaleb DuBose, 2019.

Troopers Jonathan O'Loughlin on Magnum and Michael Crowley on Sarge, 2014.

Troopers Dan Doiron and Peter Holman doing public relations at the beach.

moved to San Diego, California. The amusement center decline had begun. By the late 1990s, the Shaheen Fun-O-Rama Park had closed and Pirates Park was close behind. With seventeen bars and no amusement center to attract families, the decline was complete. The Frolics sat closed, empty and left to decay, and was finally torn down in 2000. There was nothing left to attract families except a few family run arcades and pizza shops. Summer rentals declined and many old cottages were replaced by high end condos. The number of clubs was down from seventeen to seven, tremendously reducing the number of visitors. This, coupled with the growth of nearby Hampton Beach, New Hampshire and the professionalization of the Salisbury Police Department, led to the reduced need for a full time state police presence in the beach center, and the summer detail came to an end in 1995. Single patrol cars were again sent from the Topsfield Barrack on weekends to assist the local police, but the once prized assignment to a summer detail at Salisbury Beach became a thing of the past. The Commonwealth still owns the Salisbury Beach State Reservation, the busiest state park in the state. Today, the state police mounted unit assigns three troopers on horseback to patrol the alcohol-free campground and beach every summer.

CAMARADERIE

For many years after the detail ended, Troopers have gotten together to share great stories about the arrests and incidents that occurred at Salisbury Beach. Every year for the past dozen years, Troopers have gotten together for a Beach Troopers Golf Tournament. It is organized by Steve Gravelle and held at the Apple Hill Golf Club in East Kingston, New Hampshire. After golf, the Troopers join together at Brown's Lobster Pool in Seabrook, New Hampshire for lobster, friendship, and libation. Non-golfers skip the golf and join the crew at Browns. The Salisbury Beach stories begin and get better over the years after a couple of beers. Some of those attending the annual Beach Troopers Golf Tournament are:

Steve Gravelle, Dick Downey, Mike Mucci, Ken Dunphy, Rob Smith, Tom Robbins, George Chaisson, Scott Pare, Rich Connelly, Ed Connolly, Steve Beaudoin, Barry Brodette, Don Kennefick, Ed Johnson, Bob Krom, Ed Horton, Bill Baker, Ken Gill, Tom Elias, John Lannon, Dave Fladger, Mike Cooney, Joe Duggan, Steve Hines, and Ron Guilmette.

2018 Golf Outing, kneeling L to R: The winning Team - Don Kennefick, Rich Connelly, Tom Elias, and Ron Guilmette. Standing: Steve Gravelle, Steve Hines, Mike Mucci, Ed Connolly, Ed Horton, Dave Fladger, Mike Cooney, Dick Downey, John Jakubowski, Steve Beaudoin and Rob Smith.

2021 Beach Troopers Golf winning Team: Rob Smith, Dick Downey, Ron Guilmette, and Ed Johnson.

2013 Beach Troopers Golf, seated front: Scott Pare, Ken Gill, Ron Guilmette, Tom Robbins. Rear: Jim Devlin, Tom Elias, George Chaisson, Rich Connelly, Rob Smith, Steve Gravelle, Dick Downey, Ed Johnson, and Ed Connolly.

2022 Lunch at Mountainview Station Restaurant, Ossipee, New Hampshire: Beach Troopers Rob Smith, Ken Dunphy, Steve Gravelle, and Ron Guilmette.

2023 Golf, seated: George Chaisson. Standing L to R: Rob Smith, Rich Connelly, Don Kennefick, Ed Johnson, Steve Gravelle, and Bob Krom.

Former Beach Trooper get together, 2019. kneeling, L to R: Tom Elias, Barry Brodette, John Lannon, Steve Hines, Scott Pare, Mike Cooney, and Ed Connolly. Standing: Steve Gravelle, Bob Krom, Dave Fladger, Rob Smith, Don Kennefick, Rich Connelly, Ron Guilmette, Dick Downey, Tom Robbins, Bill Baker, Ken Gill, and Joe Duggan.

Index

A

Ali, Muhammad 31
Alvino, Steve 4, 41, 42
Amadeo, Ed 42
Ambrose, Greg 42
Amodeo, Eddie 4, 42
Anka, Paul 43
Arena, Dominic 22
Armstrong, Louis 43

B

Bailey, Warren 28
Baker, Bill 45, 46
Barnard, Beverly Donahue 4
Barry, Francis X. 16, 19
Barry, Richard 27
Bean, Leward L. "Joe" 10
Beaudoin, Steve 38, 39, 40, 41, 45
Beaupre, Charles T. 4
Belanger, Dick 4
Belanger, Sue 4
Bellanti, Ronald (Ron) 31, 33
Beloff, Paul 27, 30
Bennett, Dean 35, 36, 37
Bennett, Tony 43
Berglund, Herbert S. 10
Bertulli, Dennis 4, 42
Birmingham, Robert J. 22, 27
Blake, John C. 9, 10, 11, 13, 15, 25
Blouin, Aime 28, 29
Boluch, Bohdan W. 20, 21
Boone, Pat 43
Bourbeau, Robert F. 10, 11, 12, 13, 16, 24
Boyd, Harry 27, 29
Brodette, Barry 41, 45, 46
Brooks, Bill 36
Brooks, Dennis 39
Burke, Walter P. 7

C

Caggiano, Vincent 27, 28
Cain, Thomas 26
Calderwood, Roger 35, 41, 42
Callahan, Donald D. 23, 27, 28
Canning, Thomas 42
Canty, James T. 27, 28, 31

Carbone, Peter 42
Carney, Leo 21
Castro, Fidel 24
Chaisson, Arthur F. 7, 8, 9, 10
Chaisson, George 39, 45
Ciampa, Giuseppe 43
Coe, Charlie 27, 28
Coffey, Thomas 39
Collins, Charles J. 10, 18
Collins, John W. 10
Congdon, Harold 5, 43
Connelly, Richard (Rich) 4, 37, 38, 45, 46
Connolly, Ed 40, 45, 46
Cooney, Mike 41, 45, 46
Cote, Hector J. 17, 19, 20, 21
Cote, Hervey 4
Credit, George 41, 42
Cronin, John J. 28, 33
Crowley, Jerry 20, 21
Crowley, Michael 44
Crowley, Richard J. 21
Crump, Jim 4
Cummings, William 28
Currier, Mike 42
Curtin, John 37, 38

D

Davis, Sammy Jr. 43
Dean, Jimmy 43
DeLesDernier, Richard (Dick) 35, 36
Desmond, Dan 18
Desmond, Ed 33, 34, 35
Devillis, Frank 42
Devlin, Jim 45
Doiron, Dan 44
Donahue, James M. 19, 20, 21
Donlon, Joseph (Joe) 41, 42
Donohue, Thomas (Tom) 37, 38
Dooling, Jeff 42
Dooling, Thomas M. 28, 32, 33
Downer, Ted 41
Downey, Dick 38, 45, 46
Downey, John 19
Driscoll, Daniel F. 15, 22
DuBose, Kaleb 43
Duggan, Joe 45, 46

Dunford, James 29
Dunphy, Kenneth (Ken) 28, 45

E

Eastman, Charlie 36
Edwards, George C. 10, 12, 13, 17, 18
Elias, Tom 39, 40, 45, 46
Ellington, Duke 43
Eng, Brian 4, 42
Eubanks, Richard 42

F

Fallon, John H. 11
Fay, Lawrence 28
Fay, Pat 29
Ferrick, Michael (Mike) 37
Fielding, George F. 7, 8
Fladger, Dave 45, 46
Fletcher, Paul 39
Foley, Maurice 19, 20, 21, 24
Follett, Robert 42
Ford, Arthur V. 7
Ford, Roger 33, 34, 35
Francis, Connie 43
French, Paul 28
Furze, Charles F. 9, 10, 11

G

Geist, Frank 11, 12, 13
Gilday, Lefty 18
Gilligan, Charles W. 21, 22
Gill, Ken 40, 45, 46
Gilman, John 27, 28, 33, 34
Grabowski, Dan 35
Grady, William 19
Gravelle, Steven (Steve) 4, 33, 34, 35, 37, 38, 39, 45, 46
Grillo, Anthony 25, 26, 27, 35
Grundy, William 19
Guilmette, Ronald (Ron) J. 4, 35, 36, 37, 38, 39, 45, 46

H

Hall, George 5
Hall, Gertrude 5
Hallice, Chester E. Jr. 27, 32
Hannigan, Francis C. 7
Harding, Larry 25

Harding, Lawrence 22
Harvey, Ted 35
Hendrigan, Rod 39
Herzog, Robert 20, 21
Hewitt, Alfred 17
Hiller, Richard (Dick) P. 25, 28, 32
Hines, Steve 45, 46
Holman, Peter 44
Horton, Ed 4, 41, 45
Houghton, George F. 15, 19, 20
Hyde, John J. 19

I

Irving, William H. 22, 25

J

Jackson, Robert T. 4
Jackson, Stan 24
Jacobs, Daniel L. 10
Jakubowski, John 45
Johnson, Ed 31, 35, 39, 45
Johnson, Ed III 4
Johnson, Edward 35
Johnston, Frederick (Fred) L. 28, 31
Jowett, Arthur 19, 27, 28, 29, 33

K

Kane, Robert 28
Kane, William 16
Keeler, Robert 27
Kelley, Ed 24
Kelley, Joseph (Joe) 18, 21, 27
Kelly, Edward 19, 21
Kennedy, John F. 19, 27
Kennedy, Ted 22
Kennefick, Donald (Don) 4, 37, 38, 39, 40, 45, 46
Killen, William B. 7, 9
Killoran, James 27
Kirk, Paul 43
Kopechne, Mary Joe 22
Kornachuck, Walter 17
Krom, Bob 4, 39, 40, 41, 45, 46
Kulik, John 16, 22, 23, 26

L

LaCasse, Donat 7, 12
Lannon, John 45, 46

LaPoint, John J. 19
Laprel, Bob 40, 41
Larson, Carl M. 15, 17, 18
LaShoto, Walter D. 15
Latham, Bruce 28, 31
Leary, Francis 27
Lewis, Richard 27, 30
Linehan, Cornelius Mike 27, 28
Linehan, Michael 28, 30
Long, Robert A. 18
Longval, Armand 26, 27, 30
Loynd, Richard (Dick) N. 22, 26, 28

M

MacDonald, Donald H. 21, 22, 26, 27
Magner, Craig 41
Mahoney, Francis 27
Mahoney, Frank 23
Manzi, Al 40, 41
Masiello, Dianne 4
Mathis, Johnny 43
Mattaliano, James 41
Mazeikus, Peter 4
McCabe, Arthur E. 9
McCann, David 43
McDonald, Richard J. "Red" 3
McKeon, Bob 4
McNulty, Thomas (Tom) 4, 31, 33
McVeigh, Frank J. Jr. 28, 29, 32
McVeigh, Gail 4
Mitchell, Robert J. 16
Monahan, Robert (Bob) F. 35, 37
Morrissey, Robert (Bob) 28, 33, 34
Morse, Grant 33
Mortimer, Philip 20, 21

Mucci, Mike 33, 34, 45
Mulligan, Edward 22
Murgia, Robert D. 18, 19, 21, 22
Murphy, Eugene L. 6, 21, 22
Murphy, Gene 22
Murphy, George 28
Murphy, John J. 20, 21, 28, 32
Murphy, Martin A. 19, 20, 21, 29
Murphy, Martin F. 29
Murphy, Peter J. 22, 27
Murphy, Thomas D. 16

N

Noone, Mike 28

O

Ober, Arthur 4, 22, 23, 24
O'Brien, Steve 36
O'Donnell, John J. 26
O'Donovan, John R. 22, 26
O'Loughlin, Jonathan 44
O'Malley, Jack 35, 36
O'Malley, John 35
O'Neil, Kevin 42
O'Neill, Richard D. 28, 32
Oteri, James V. 26

P

Page, Patti 43
Pagley, Dana 40
Panacopoulos, Ross 41
Pare, Scott 40, 41, 45, 46
Perry, Paul 41
Peterson, Paul A. 16, 17
Peterson, Thomas 18, 19
Phair, Mike 35
Powers, John J. 7, 8
Powers, Richard 26, 27
Powers, William F. 33
Procopio, Dave 4

Q

Qualters, Thomas J. 7, 8

R

Raye, Martha 43
Reddish, Harry 21
Ridge, Patrick T. 7
Rizos, David 40, 41
Robbins, Thomas (Tom) 37, 38, 39, 45, 46
Robbins, Tom 40
Roche, Joe 36
Rooney, Mickey 43
Roosevelt, Eleanor 8
Roosevelt, Franklin D. 7, 8
Ryan, Kristen 4

S

Sabanski, Albert (Al) 22, 23
Sadler, John T. 16
Sargent, Francis 33
Savage, Roland 10
Scarth, Sydney (Sid) 21, 22
Schlesinger, Arthur M. 27
Schneiderhan, Richard 26
Schroeder, Walter A. 18
Scott, Arthur J. Jr. 28, 32
Shaheen, Roger 33
Shea, Michael 12, 13
Silva, Patrick 4, 42
Simpson, John 35, 36
Smith, Elizabeth Coulson 5
Smith, James P. 5
Smith, Rob 40
Smith, Robert (Rob) B. 7, 8, 38, 39, 45, 46
Stewart, William 22, 24
Stone, Joseph 28, 29, 42
Strout, George 26
Sullivan, Edward J. 12, 13
Sullivan, Henry E. 4, 28, 32

Sullivan, Joseph W. 19, 23
Sullivan, Robert G. 27, 28, 30
Sullivan, William J. 16, 30
Swanson, Gustave R. 13

T

Tammaro, Carmen V. 28, 30
Tarsook, Charlie 36
Toomey, James Michael 39, 40
Twomey, Dan 33, 35

U

Uzdawinis, Bronius 18

V

Vets, Carl J. 24, 27

W

Wall, George 22
Walsh, Basil 24, 27
Walsh, Thomas (Tom) 33, 37
Welcome, Alfred 28
Wersoski, Stephen S. 16
Wicks, Dan 42
Williams, Ruth Olive 20
Woick, Alexander (Albie) 9, 10, 13
Woodward, Robert C. 22

Y

Young, James (Jim) 37

Z

Zani, Al 40
Zuk, Julian 13, 15
Zuk, Peter 16
Zundell, Gerald 28